TEXAS LEGENDS ★ BOOK 3

Texas Legends: Book One *Last Gun*
Book Two *Captain Jack*

Rawhider

The Story
of Print Olive

GENE SHELTON

A DOUBLE D WESTERN
DOUBLEDAY
New York   London   Toronto   Sydney   Auckland

41600

A Double D Western
PUBLISHED BY DOUBLEDAY
a division of Bantam Doubleday Dell Publishing Group, Inc.
666 Fifth Avenue, New York, New York 10103

Double D Western, Doubleday,
and the portrayal of the letters DD
are trademarks of Doubleday, a division of
Bantam Doubleday Dell Publishing Group, Inc.

Library of Congress Cataloging-in-Publication Data

Shelton, Gene.
Rawhider: the story of Print Olive/by Gene Shelton.—1st ed.
p.   cm.—(Texas legends; bk. 3)
1. Olive, Isom Prentice, 1840–1886—Fiction. 2. Texas
History—1846–1950—Fiction. I. Title. II. Series.
PS3569.H39364R3   1992
813′.54—dc20   91-33400
CIP

ISBN 0-385-41901-5
Printed in the United States of America
June 1992
First Edition

To Shirley Jo—

World champion sister, educator, ranch wife, and a good hand on horseback—this work is dedicated with love.

FOREWORD

This is a work of fiction based on the life of Isom Prentice (Print) Olive, one of the Old West's deadliest gunmen and cattle barons whose legend lives for the most part in conflicting accounts and relative obscurity.

Many of the individuals portrayed in this work actually existed, but the reader should draw no conclusions as to their actual characters, motivations or actions on the basis of this story.

Numerous other characters and events herein are purely the creation of the author.

Every effort has been made, within the framework of the fiction novel, to portray as accurately as possible the actual dates, locations and sequence of events that shaped the life of Print Olive.

ACKNOWLEDGMENTS

The author wishes to express his gratitude to the many historians, library staff members, fellow Western writers and others without whose assistance this work would not have been possible.

Special thanks is offered to Mrs. Clara Scarborough of Georgetown, Texas, who was gracious enough to share her knowledge of the Olive family with the author. Mrs. Scarborough's book *Land of Good Water* was an invaluable guide to the early days of Williamson County and Print Olive's years in Texas.

Thanks also to the staff of the East Texas State University library in Commerce, Texas, who were kind enough to interrupt busy schedules to lend a hand in research.

The author also is indebted to Leon C. Metz of El Paso, Texas, whose brief biography of Print Olive in the fine book *The Shooters* inspired this story, and to the late Marie Sandoz, whose book *The Cattlemen* helped fill in numerous blanks in the life of Print Olive.

Other valuable sources included Jay Robert Nash's *Bloodletters and Badmen;* Teddy Blue Abbott and Helena Huntington Smith's *We Pointed Them North;* and the many historical accounts of Hood's Brigade and the men who fought with Hood in the Civil War.

—GENE SHELTON
Sulphur Springs, Texas

ONE

Virginia
October 1864

The pain had come to life again.

The seed planted in torn flesh spread its roots and thrust tendrils of thorns through the leg of the tall, gaunt man who limped along the dusty road at the edge of the battered column of Confederate prisoners.

Isom Prentice Olive, First Texas Volunteers, Hood's Brigade, Confederate States of America, tried to ignore the pain along with the bite of autumn wind through the remnants of faded butternut cloth that once had been a uniform. The rough material scraped against ridged scars on his right shoulder and upper back, the legacy of a canister shell in the desperate battle for the place called Gettysburg. The musket ball that seeded the pain in his left thigh was a souvenir of The Wilderness.

It was getting to the point, he thought, where a man could follow the course of the war just by counting the scars on Print Olive's body. *At least, by God,* he told himself, *we dealt out more than we took and we took a hell of a lot; the First Texas never quit a fight—*

A sudden stab of new pain shattered the thought.

Print spun to face the Union soldier who had jabbed his rifle muzzle into Print's still-sore shoulder. "Move along, Reb." The guard's thumb rested on the hammer of the Springfield. His thin mouth twisted in a sneer. A flare of rage pushed away Print's pain. He lunged forward, slapped away the muzzle of the rifle and cocked a clubbed fist. A hand clamped onto his arm before he could swing.

"Easy, Print," Deacon Scruggs's voice near his ear said, "don't give the blueleg an excuse. We've been through too much together to get killed now."

The Union guard stumbled back a step, shaken by the unexpected attack.

"You Yankee sonofabitch." Print's voice was low, hard and cold. "You come at me again and I'll stick that rifle up your ass and pull the trigger."

The guard recovered from the shock, sputtered in outrage and thumbed back the hammer of the rifle. A Union sergeant sprinted to the guard and shoved the rifle aside. "Back off, Private! Show these men the respect they deserve! We're here to swap prisoners, not to shoot them!"

Deacon's grip was still firm on Print's arm. "Let it go, Print. It's not worth it."

The Union sergeant turned to Print. "Your friend's right, soldier," he said. "This war's nearly over. There's no sense in getting killed now, for nothing."

Print willed his muscles to relax. His anger was checked more by weakness and exhaustion than by reason. Thirty months of war, almost constant hunger, cold and heat, two wounds, and half a year in a Union prison camp had taken the edge from his body, if not his temper. He fixed a steady glare on the young private. "The next time we meet I'll kill you," he said. "And if it's not in this war, by God, you have my personal invitation to come to Williamson County, Texas, to settle up. Just ask for Print Olive whenever you get tired of living."

The restraining hand fell away from Print's arm. "Come on, Print, let it slide."

Print sighed, turned from the Union soldier and let Deacon Scruggs set the pace as they rejoined the ranks of Confederate prisoners. Deacon was almost a head shorter than Print but packed a lot of muscle into a short frame. He had the powerful arms and hands of a blacksmith, a barrel chest and legs that seemed stubby beneath his massive trunk. A bandage crusted with dried blood covered his left eye.

Deacon twisted his head to look at Print with his remaining eye. "I reckon that sergeant's right, Print," he said. There was sadness in his words. "The Yankees are likely gonna win this war. But we give 'em a helluva scrap along the way."

Print grunted an agreement, still struggling to contain his anger, and walked in silence for a hundred yards. Then he glanced at his companion. "Deacon," he said, "I'm tired, I'm hungry, and I'm hurting. But I'll promise you this right now. No man is ever again going to tell me when I'm whipped. I've been pushed around and ordered around for the last time. And they'll have to kill me before they take my guns away again."

TWO

Williamson County, Texas
August 1865

A gentle southwest breeze flattened the gray-white smoke from the open charcoal pits where slabs of beef, quartered pigs and whole chickens dripped juices onto the smoldering embers below. The scent set Jim Olive's mouth watering as he looked over the growing crowd.

Jim sometimes had trouble accepting the idea that more than twenty years had passed since he, his wife Julia and their two children, Elizabeth and Print, had settled at the Lawrence Chapel community on Brushy Creek. *It just doesn't seem that time can get away from a man that fast,* he thought. But it had.

Overall, it had been a good twenty years, Jim had to admit. The store he had founded in Lawrence Chapel was doing well. His holdings in land and cattle were sufficient to feed his wife and their nine children. In fact, Jim Olive was a wealthy man, at least in cash-strapped Texas terms. The land and the store were paid for, free and clear, and he had hard cash in the bank. Not a lot, but enough. And enough was a lot more than most of the state's merchants and farmers had.

Now, Print, the eldest son, was twenty-five and a grown man, home safe from the war. He had almost recovered from his wounds and his six-foot frame had fleshed out to its normal hundred-ninety solid pounds. This gathering served a twofold purpose, both on Print's behalf; to celebrate his return and to welcome his bride, Louise, into the family.

Jim's gaze drifted over the crowd. As was usual with a gathering hosted by the Olives, almost half the Williamson County populace was on hand. Not all of them were friends or even acquaintances. Some came just for the food and drink. Jim didn't mind feeding a hungry stranger and his family once in a while.

No one would have any trouble picking the Olive boys out in the crowd, he thought. Print, Jay, Ira, Marion and even young Bob carried their mother's stamp. Julia Ann Brashear Olive couldn't deny them. They all favored the dark-skinned, dark-eyed and handsome part Cherokee woman who had helped Jim Olive build a comfortable living from the loamy soil, thick brush and timber of central Texas. *If I never did anything else right in my life,* Jim thought, *at least I picked the best woman any man could want to share a life with.*

He wasn't so sure about Print's new wife. His eyes narrowed as he watched Print and Louise greet the latest arrivals. Louise was barely five feet tall, slender, delicate almost to the point of appearing frail. She looked as though she might break in a sudden gust of wind. Her eyes frequently held the look of a frightened doe. Jim knew her life hadn't been an easy one. Orphaned as a young girl and raised by her widower grandfather on a hard-scrabble farm a few miles from town, Louise had known little but want during her young life. If dowries still mattered, Jim thought, she would have been out of luck. A couple of home-made housedresses and one Sunday church outfit wouldn't buy a girl much of a man. Now she had her man. But Jim wasn't sure she was strong enough to survive Print Olive.

Print had always been wild, even as a young boy. Print's quick temper and a stubborn streak wider than Brushy Creek in the rainy season had landed him more than a few stroppings behind the woodpile. *There should have been more trips to that woodpile,* Jim thought; *maybe I could have beaten some sense into Print if I'd set my mind to it.* Even as the thought formed, Jim Olive dismissed it. He'd done the best he could, what with Julia always taking up for Print, trying to keep the boy's misdeeds hidden from Jim as much as possible. Print had always been her favorite. In the mother's eyes her eldest son could do no wrong. "He has spirit," was her dismissal for Print's transgressions.

That spirit had led Print, at age ten, to beat a boy two years older and fifteen pounds heavier to a bleeding wreck in the dust of the churchyard over some insult. The older boy never fully regained the sight in one eye. Jim had thrashed Print, more for fighting on the Lord's land than for the fight itself. Eventually, Jim came to realize that punishment seemed only to make the boy more headstrong and moody. He gave up on the trips to the woodpile.

Jim had hoped the passing years would tone down Print's temper. They hadn't. Neither had the war. If anything, the War Between the States had sharpened that temper to a razor edge. A man did well these days to walk soft around Print Olive.

Most young men returning from battle bought a new pair of boots or a new hat as soon as they hit Texas soil. Print's first purchase had been a Remington New Model Army forty-four handgun, the second a Henry repeating rifle and the third a bottle of whiskey. It was not, Jim knew, a good sign.

"God give you strength, Louise Olive," Jim whispered toward the small auburn-haired woman standing beside Print, "because I fear you're going to need it with my son."

The clanging of the cook's triangle put an end to Jim Olive's musings. The crowd surged toward the cooking pits and nearby tables covered with fresh vegetables, steaming bread, pies, cakes and fruit. Jim rejoined his guests, pausing frequently to shake the hand of a new arrival. For now it was enough to enjoy good company and good food. Tomorrow would be soon enough for a talk with Print . . .

Isom Prentice Olive leaned against the corral gate, his gaze drifting over the handful of saddle horses as they squealed, bit and kicked at each other over grain in the feed troughs. He glanced up and nodded a greeting as Jim Olive stepped alongside and propped a foot on the lower rail of the gate.

The two men stood in silence for a moment, watching the horses sort out the pecking order for feeding time. It was a ritual that had been followed through the ages since the first domestication of the animal. Print dug a tobacco pouch from a shirt pocket, rolled a cigarette and fired it with a match scratched across a fence rail. "You wanted to talk, Pa?" he said.

"Yes, son. I'd like to know what your plans are now that you've a wife to look after."

Print turned to his father, squinting through the cigarette smoke. "Simple enough, Pa. I'm going to get rich."

Jim stared at his son for a moment, startled by the simple declaration. There was no sign of excitement or indecision in Print's black eyes, just a calm, deep confidence.

"Well, Print," Jim said, "I always have admired ambition in a man. But we've got plenty—"

"Pa," Print interrupted, "you may be satisfied with what we've got. Satisfied with a good farm, a half section of grass, and trading flour and sugar for pennies. It's not enough for me. I want to see the day come that when Print Olive talks, people listen."

Jim Olive reached for his battered pipe. "I suppose you've got this all worked out? Getting rich doesn't just happen to a man, you know."

Print stubbed his cigarette butt against a corner post. "Cattle," he said. "I've talked some with Dudley and J. W. Snyder. They know cattle. They trailed many a beef from Williamson County to the Confederacy during the war."

Jim nodded as he stoked his pipe. "The Snyders are good men. Good neighbors. I've always trusted Dudley's judgment in particular. But cattle? Print, they're not worth two bits."

"Not now, maybe. But Dudley smells a big market," Print said. "There's already a shortage of beef back east. In a year or two, Yankees are going to be yelping for steak at any price. Even Texas steak. That means money. Lots of it. I'm going to get my share and then some."

Jim fired the pipe, sucked at the stem and winced at the bite of the raw burley against his tongue. He broke the match, felt the head from habit to make sure it was out, then ground it into the dirt with the toe of his low-heeled shoe. "It takes money to make money these days, Print. I can help some, and I've saved your share of profits from the store and farm while you were gone—"

"Pa—"

"—Of course, I got stuck with a lot of worthless Confederate paper and some bad debts, but I think there might be a couple hundred to spare—"

Print put a hand on his father's shoulder. "Pa, listen to me. I've got the seed money I need already."

Jim stared at his son for a few heartbeats, confused. Nobody came out of the Confederate Army with hard cash in their pockets. "Where'd you get it, Print?"

A slight smile touched Print's lips. "I got most of it from the Yanks, Pa. I learned early in the war that when we overran a Yank position some of them carried money. Union paper, even gold and silver. I made it a point to stop long enough to relieve them of it."

Jim's jaw dropped. "You robbed the dead?"

Print shrugged. "They didn't need it anymore. And after the prisoner exchange when they sent me to garrison duty in New Orleans, I spent some off-duty hours teaching the locals how to play poker. It added up. I won't need your money."

Jim suppressed a shudder. He couldn't imagine stealing money from the dead, but it didn't seem to faze Print in the least. He sighed. "Even if you have some money, Print," he said, "there's other problems, too. Like getting cattle and grass to graze them."

Print dropped his hand from his father's shoulder and reached again for his tobacco pouch. "That's no problem, Pa. I just take what I need." He gestured with the tobacco sack toward the southwest. "Texas may be poor as lizard piss where hard cash is concerned, and the damn blueleg carpetbaggers who've moved in on us want to keep it that way. What they haven't seen yet is that Texas is covered up in cows. There's thousands of them running wild in the brush. A man who can catch them and brand them owns them."

"And land? Cows need a lot of grass."

"Hell, Pa." Print's smile was without humor. He tapped the butt of the Remington holstered at his hip. "I'll just take that, too." Print finished rolling the cigarette, fired it and exhaled the smoke through his nostrils. "We've got the land here and my claim next to it. That's a start. There's several sections of state school land close by. No reason I can't use it to run cows."

Jim's brow furrowed. "But Print, there's already some folks settled on that land. It's not yours."

"It will be, Pa. I learned a few things in the war. For one, the man with the best gun and the balls to use it gets what he wants. For another, I'm through taking orders for the rest of my life.

From now on, I'll give them." Print's black eyes glittered. "I'll just ask the squatters to move on."

"What if they don't?"

"Then I'll run down any man who stands in my way."

"Even me?"

"Don't push me to that choice, Pa. We've had our differences in the past. We may have one or two more. But we're family—and this is something I've got to do."

Print abruptly turned and strode back toward the main house. Jim sucked at the toothmarked stem of his old pipe and watched his son walk away, his long strides raising puffs of dust. Only a slight limp remained from the war wound. *God help us all,* he thought, *that boy's serious, and there isn't a thing I could say or do to stop him.*

Boggy Creek
October 1865

Print Olive shifted his weight in the saddle and wiped the sweat from his eyes with a torn shirt sleeve. He was breathing almost as hard as the lathered brown gelding between his knees.

His leg ached from the impact of a heavy horn. He could almost feel the skin begin to turn from red to purple beneath the thick leather leggings. It could have been worse, he thought. It could have been the tip of a horn that hit him when the cow fought the tie ropes.

In the near distance he could still hear the brush pop as the longhorn fought her way through the thicket, a fresh Olive brand on her left hip. There were a sizable number like her now, from weanling calves to full-grown, tough, ornery bulls with horn spans six feet or more wide. None of them had come easy.

Print leaned forward and patted the brown's neck, letting the animal know it had done its job well. Blood trickled from the gelding's shoulder where a horntip had nicked the skin.

"Well, Buckshot," he said to the horse, "that one was a little meaner than most, but we were meaner than her. Maybe Pa's right. It takes a damn fool on a dumb horse to tackle a full-grown longhorn maverick alone."

He reached for his tobacco pouch as he waited for the circle-shaped running iron to cool in the dust where he had dropped it before flipping the catch rope from the cow's horns and loosening the tie ropes. It had taken the cow a few seconds to figure out that she could stand. By that time Print was back in the saddle, ready to dodge if she charged. She hadn't.

Buckshot snorted the dust from his nostrils and shook his head, rattling the bit and curb chain. Then the horse's ears abruptly came up, alert and pointed to the right. Print let his hand drop to the butt of the holstered Remington. He kneed the brown to the edge of the small clearing where he would have a good field of fire.

"Print! You in there?"

Print relaxed at the sound of the familiar bass voice. "Ride on in, Jim!" he called.

Print grinned as Jim Kelly rode into the clearing. Sweat poured down his ebony face. Kelly wore his own fresh scars of the day's work. Thorn cuts and welts from whipping branches crisscrossed his broad black face. A trace of blood seeped from a scrape along a thick forearm.

Jim Kelly was two inches shorter than Print's six feet, but he looked bigger, with a massive chest, powerful legs and hands that could crush a green bois d'arc apple or a man's windpipe with equal ease. Wiry eyebrows bunched beneath a scarred forehead and above a once-broken nose. Kelly had been with the Olives since he was a skinny-assed kid. Now he was a grown man, a couple of years Print's junior. He was a top cowhand and horse breaker, and he also was one of the best men with a pistol Print had ever seen.

Kelly had a habit of grinding his teeth when he was angry. A man could hear the grit of those molars six feet away, and when Jim Kelly gnashed his teeth and rolled his eyes upward until only the whites showed, any thinking man who happened to be in Jim's way suddenly remembered a place he had to be—in a hurry.

Jim Kelly, Print thought, was a good man to have alongside in either ranch work or trouble time. He usually made it a point to

keep Kelly close by. Already, the big black man was known as
"Print's Bad Nigger" throughout Williamson County, and especially among the farmers and small ranchers Print and Jim had
invited to vacate the state lands now claimed as Olive property.
Kelly's temperament was a near match to Print's. It didn't take
much to set him off. And when he ground his teeth, rolled his
eyes and reached for that big Colt Dragoon at his waist, it was
something to behold. Print secretly hoped Jim never had occasion to grind those teeth at him.

Some Southerners thought it odd, or even revolting, that a
Confederate and a black man could share a strong bond. The
friendship between the two had been forged years ago when
they were both reckless youths, and usually both in trouble with
their fathers for transgressions real or imagined. The bond had
been honed in mutual respect and, of late, polished by loyalty to
the Olive brand.

"Catch up with that one, Jim?"

"Caught the slab-sided sumbitch," Kelly groused. "Like to not
got him turned loose, but we got another critter in the clan. You
make out all right?"

Print nodded and tossed the tobacco sack to Kelly. "Man who
says it's easy catching wild cattle in this damn brush never has
had the pleasure. But we're gaining on them. Pretty soon there'll
be an Olive cow behind every post oak in the county. Besides,
where else could a man have such a good time on a Saturday
afternoon?"

Jim Kelly licked the edge of the cigarette paper, folded it over
and stroked it in place, twisted the ends and tossed the makings
back to Print with a grin. "With Maryann Conklin in her old
man's hayloft, I'd reckon."

Print chuckled. "Can't argue with that, Jim." He'd been in the
Conklin hayloft a time or two himself, before the war. Maryann
was the color of creamed coffee, with long, strong legs and a
knee problem. She couldn't keep them together. It was a nice
combination.

The two men smoked in silence for a few minutes before Print
retrieved his now cool branding ring and remounted.

"Want to chase some more cows?" Kelly asked.

Print shook his head. "Horses are about worn down. Let's

head on back. I want to stop off at that hog farmer's place on the way." Print's eyes narrowed. "He's been a pain in the butt. You'd think a grown man could savvy English. I guess we'll just have to draw him a picture in the dirt."

Print saw the flicker of anticipation in Kelly's dark eyes. He kneed Buckshot toward a narrow opening in the thicket. The thrill of the chase and the danger of the catch faded as he rode, and with its passing Print's mood darkened.

It seemed there was always something to threaten the start he had made on his ranch with his sweat and blood. Hundreds of cattle now wore the Olive brand. Print, Ira and Marion had their own claims adjoining their father's holdings. Now, the state land to the west of Lawrence Chapel was the key to Print's future. And a damn hog farmer had plopped himself and his dirty brood down on the best spring-fed creek around, fouling the soil with his plow and the water with his pig piss. *This time, by God, he'll know we're not whistling in the wind,* Print vowed silently.

Print had been smelling the place for a good mile before he pulled the brown to a stop before a half-dugout, half-picket shack stuck haphazardly against a low hill. His nose wrinkled in revolt at the powerful stink from a couple dozen hogs crowded into the muck of a log pen only a few steps from the shack. He glanced at Kelly and saw his own disgust mirrored in the cowboy's grimace. Print eased the Henry from its boot and rested the weapon across the pommel of his saddle.

"Hansen!" Print yelled. "Get your butt out here!"

The crude door of the shack opened a crack, framing half a thin, wary face. The hog farmer's visible eye was wide in obvious fear. "Leave us alone, Olive!" The man's voice quavered as he called the challenge.

"Get out here now or I'll burn the place with you in it!" Print's voice was taut with raw anger and contempt.

The door swung open on leather hinges. Hansen stepped through the doorway. His stoop-shouldered frame seemed to shrink even more as his gaze darted from Print to the big black man. Behind Hansen a thin, weary-looking woman stood just inside the door, her stringy hair falling over the shoulders of a soiled and patched dress. Two small children huddled behind her, equally scrawny and equally afraid of the two men on the big horses.

"Hansen," Print said, "I told you four days ago to clear off Olive land and take your damn stinking pigs with you. You got a hearing problem, Hansen?"

"You—you can't—" Hansen's voice trembled as he stammered "—run us out. We—got rights to this land same as anybody—"

Print lifted the Henry and cocked the hammer. "You have no rights to anything, Hansen. Except your life, if you're smart enough to save it."

"I ain't goin', Olive." The farmer made an effort to square his shoulders. "You can't run us off! We ain't takin' nothin' from you —and I ain't a'scared of you!"

Print's eyes narrowed. His gaze locked on Hansen's face until the farmer squirmed in the lengthening silence. Hansen tried to stare down Print and failed. Print breathed a heavy sigh. "Not only are you a defiler of the land, Hansen, you're a piss-poor liar, too. I'm not an unreasonable man. I'll give you two more days to clear out. But I'm going to let you know that this time I mean business." Print nodded toward Kelly. "This big nigger here doesn't like hogs one bit, Hansen. His little brother was eaten by a pair of sows."

Kelly glared toward the pig pen, growled low in his throat and ground his teeth. The sound was like two rough stones grated together. He rolled his eyes back in his head and dropped his hand to the grip of the Dragoon. Hansen's eyes widened until a man could have set a coffee cup on either one, Print noted with satisfaction.

"Only thing he hates worse than pigs is pig farmers." Print shrugged. "I don't think I can keep him under control much longer, Hansen."

Kelly growled again and yanked the Dragoon from the holster. He cocked the revolver and whirled his horse toward the pig pen. Hansen cringed at the first pistol blast and the death squeal of a hog.

"No! Olive—stop him—them hogs is all I got—"

"I can't stop him now, Hansen. You had your chance and you were too stone-dumb to take it."

Tears flowed down Hansen's pinched face as the echoes of the sixth shot died away. Print never took his eyes off Hansen. The hog farmer made no attempt to reach for a weapon. Print didn't know if Hansen even owned a gun or had the nerve to try to use one, but a desperate man was the most dangerous beast alive.

Jim Kelly reined his mount back alongside Print, tamping a fresh charge into a chamber of the Dragoon. His eyes narrowed to mere slits as he stared at Hansen.

"Now, Hansen," Print said, "I want no more truck with hogs on my land. If you and your brood aren't gone next time I come by, I'll let this nigger here kill the rest of the hogs. Then I'll let him shoot you and burn your shack to the ground." Print shook his head in mock sadness. "Be mighty tough on your woman and kids, Hansen. Maybe you aren't much, but you're all they've got. Think it over. While you start packing."

Print backed his horse a few feet, then reined the animal about, convinced that Hansen didn't have the courage to brace him, even with a back shot. If he tried, Jim Kelly would kill the whole bunch, and Hansen knew it. The two men rode in silence for a quarter of an hour. Then Jim Kelly chuckled and glanced at Print.

"Hogs et my brother, did they?"

Print shrugged. "Could have happened. Hansen believed it." He grinned at the black man. "Jim, I'll be damned if you don't even scare me just a little bit sometimes with that act of yours."

"Saves some killin'. Not that it matters much. You reckon he'll leave?"

Print nodded. "He'll leave. I know Hansen's kind. He hasn't got the guts to get a gun and face up, to fight for his own. That's the difference between us and them, Jim. That's why they'll always be poor and we'll be rich."

Kelly chuckled, a deep baritone rumble from the massive chest. "Now that's something to think on, bein' rich. Then maybe I can afford me something besides Maryann Conklin." The smile faded from Kelly's lips. "Trouble is, we got to stay alive in the meantime. You know well as I do who put that hog farmer up to movin' in on Olive land."

Print's jaw knotted as his anger bubbled back to the surface. "Turk Turner. Someday Turner and I will have it out, Jim. Bet on me when the time comes."

Jim Kelly fell silent, leaving Print to stew in his own hate for Turk Turner. Turner was a neighbor of sorts. He ran cattle at the eastern edge of Jim Olive's spread. Bad feelings between Turner and Print Olive went back years. Nobody could even remember now what started the personal feud. What started it didn't matter now, Kelly knew. It was who finished it that counted.

Kelly broke the silence with a loud snort. "I can still smell that damn pig farm, Print. I sure hope Ma's not feedin' me pork chops tonight."

THREE

Lawrence Chapel
October 1866

Louise Olive sat amid the tumble of bedclothes, her back braced against the heavy oak headboard, fingers toying with the tangles of auburn hair that fell across her shoulder onto a bare breast. A growing anxiety pushed through the lassitude that followed their early morning lovemaking as she watched her husband knot his black string tie and reach for the gunbelt on its peg by the bedroom door.

"Print, please," she said softly, almost begging, "stay here—with me—today. It seems you're never home—"

"Quit whining, woman," Print snapped. Anger flared in his dark eyes as he turned to face Louise. "I've been busting my butt building our ranch, and by God, I've earned a little fun. I sure haven't had much around here."

Louise felt the sudden constriction of fear and hurt in her throat. Tears stung the corners of her eyes. "Print, I—I don't know what I've done wrong—"

Print slammed a fist into the bedside table hard enough to send the water pitcher skittering. "For Christ's sake, Louise! Don't tell me what to do! I swore I'd never again take orders from any man and I sure as hell won't take them from a woman!" He glared at her as Louise cringed against the pillow, then slowly unclenched his fist. "For the first time in your life you've got good clothes, three meals a day and money in your purse. You ought to be satisfied with that."

"Print, please don't be angry." Louise tried to control the tremor in her voice. "You've been a good husband, a good provider. I'm not whining. It's just that I don't want to see you hurt, and Round Rock is a dangerous place."

The rage drained from Print's face as quickly as it had appeared. He reached out and stroked her forearm. "I know, Louise. I'll be careful." He let his hand drop to grip the Remington. "There won't be any trouble at Round Rock that I can't handle." His lips lifted in a small, tight grin. Louise saw no mirth in the half smile. "I'll be back by noon tomorrow."

Louise Olive held back her tears until the door closed behind Print. She sat and stared at the door, her cheeks glistening. She had heard ridicule all her life. She had never been able to please her grandfather, who seemed to blame her for her parents' death, as if the lung fever had been her fault. But sharp words still hurt. Especially from Print.

Louise knew that understanding Print was beyond her limited abilities. He could be as gentle as a spring rain or as brutal as a winter blizzard, and his moods often changed in a heartbeat. She had spoken the truth when she said he was a good provider. She no longer knew poverty and hunger and want, and soon they would be moving to the new ranch house to the west of his father's holdings. She would have her own home by spring. That made up for some of the other times. Print was a hard worker. Better than two thousand cattle now carried the Olive brand. He was also a good lover, when the mood for tenderness struck him. Other times it was quick, almost brutal.

Louise tried to blame the war for changing Print, but she knew that was a lame excuse at best. He had been moody, often quarrelsome and sometimes violent long before the war. It was as though Print were one of those Manila hemp ropes he favored, sometimes stretched to the near-breaking point, relaxed and pliable at other times.

Louise Olive wiped a hand across her damp cheeks and squared her shoulders. She might never understand Print Olive. She might even fear him. But with Print, she knew there would never be the pain of the empty belly, the humiliation of being poor. And if she were careful of her tongue and alert to his moods, perhaps he would never hit her, the way some men did their wives. He could give her something she wanted deeply, a future and a family. Louise breathed a silent prayer that this morning he had given her a son.

Perhaps, she thought, complete happiness was never to be hers. But with Print her chance for at least partial contentment was within reach. Perhaps that was all an orphan girl should expect. It would be so much easier to accept, though, if it weren't for one simple and at times painful fact: She was in love with Isom Prentice Olive.

Print Olive sat at a table at the end of the bar in Blakely's Round Rock Emporium, glowering at a half-empty whiskey bottle before him. Normally, Ned Blakely's good Kentucky bourbon put Print in a mellow mood. Today was different.

The cards weren't falling for Print, and it wasn't because he was bucking a marked deck. It was a fair game, as near as he could tell. He was down thirty dollars—about six or seven head of prime steers by the Texas standard of measurement. He fanned his hand, saw nothing promising and folded when the man to his left opened. He ignored the play of the hand and gazed around the Emporium. The place was crowded, as it usually was on a Saturday evening. Blakely didn't cut his drinks. The games were honest and there were no professional gamblers allowed. The Emporium was the gathering spot of cattlemen and their hired hands, merchants, drovers and drifters, and the occasional farmer with the price of a drink in his pocket.

Jim Kelly leaned against the end of the bar a few feet from Print's table, a mug of beer clutched in a big left hand. His right hand never strayed far from the Dragoon at his belt.

Print frowned toward three men dressed in range garb clustered at the bar. They had been drinking steadily when Print arrived and showed no signs of slowing down. Their voices kept getting louder as the evening wore on. The racket put even more of an edge on Print's raw mood.

"I tell you one damn thing for sure," one of the men said, his voice carrying clearly to Print, "we whipped the dog crap outta them Johnny Rebs at Rocky Ridge, sure enough." The speaker was a lanky, sandy-haired man with a drooping mustache and a Colt New Army pistol slung in a hip holster.

Print felt the color rise in his neck. He shoved his chair back, stood and eased his way to the bar within an arm's length of the speaker.

"I tell you fair, old Hood's boys went off a'yelpin' and a'runnin', they did. Hell, I thought the First Texas was supposed to be a tough outfit—"

"They were, Yank," Print interrupted, "and you are one of the biggest damn liars ever to come down the pike."

The sandy-haired man turned toward Print and blinked whiskey-blurred eyes. "What you say?"

"I said you're a liar. You deaf as well?" Print's tone was low, hard. "The First Texas was the outfit kicking ass at Rocky Ridge. We never saw anything of you damn bluelegs but the seat of your britches from that first charge on. I wouldn't be surprised if you're not carrying a Confederate rifle ball in your butt to this day."

The man cursed and stabbed a hand toward the Colt. Print thrust out his left hand and grabbed the man's wrist, trapping the hand against the weapon and gunbelt. At the same instant he hammered a hard right fist to the bridge of the man's nose. The Yank's head snapped back. Print jerked the man's hand aside, pulled the Colt from the holster and slammed the weapon against the man's temple. The tall man sagged against the bar.

One of the Yank's companions reached toward his waistband.

"Touch the pistol and you're dead, friend," Jim Kelly's voice rumbled. Print glanced to his left. Kelly had the Dragoon out and cocked, its impressive bore pointed toward the other two men. Print forgot about those two. They would cause no problem. He ripped the barrel of the pistol across the Yank's forehead. The blade sight sliced the skin to the bone; the thin man's knees went slack. Print held him erect and whipped the pistol barrel across his head and face, cursing with every blow.

A powerful hand clamped Print's wrist and shoved the pistol to the bar top. "That's enough, Print!"

Print struggled to free his hand until Ned Blakely's voice penetrated his fury. "No need to kill him. He's learned his lesson."

Print fought Blakely's grip another few seconds, but couldn't break free. Finally he stepped back, let the unconscious and bleeding man slump to the floor, then turned to the other two.

"How about you?" Print growled. "You got an opinion about the First Texas, too?"

The smaller of the men raised his hands, palms outward. "I got no quarrel with you, mister," he said. "Rusty there was out of line. Sometimes he pops off when he gets drunk. Hell, he wasn't even in the army. Neither side. His brother was. Union. Got killed at Gettysburg."

"Well, this one's been in the damn war now," Print said. He dropped the blood-spattered revolver on the downed man's chest. "You boys get this pile of dog shit out of my sight before I lose my temper."

The smaller man knelt at the battered rider's side, then looked up at Print. "He's still alive, mister. But that don't mean it's over. This man here's Turk Turner's nephew. Turk ain't gonna like this much."

A fresh wave of rage washed over Print. He glared at the young cowboy. "Son, I don't give a damn if he's the twin brother to Jesus Christ. Get him away from here before I decide to kill him. And you tell Turk Turner if he wants to take it up, he'll know where I am. Print Olive's not a hard man to find."

The cowboy's eyes widened in surprise. "You're Print Olive? I've heard about you and your nigger gunman over there. I ain't sayin' I ain't scared of you, but Turner ain't. You'll be seein' him, I reckon."

"That," Print said, "would pleasure me a lot, son." He started to turn away, then glanced back over his shoulder. "By the way, son," he said casually, "that man over there's name is Jim Kelly. You'll notice he's still got that big pistol in his hand. He might be a nigger, but he's a little touchy about who calls him one. Might keep that in mind."

Print spun about and strode toward the door. "Come along, Jim," he called over his shoulder. "Round Rock's getting to be a boil on my butt."

Middle Yegua Creek
December 1866

Print Olive tied the last hitch in the rope securing the field-dressed deer to the pack on the nervous sorrel's back. The smell of the buck's blood made the sorrel skittish, but Print knew he'd get used to it within a mile.

It had been a good hunt. The first real cold snap of the year had put the deer on the move. The buck he had dropped was thick in the neck from the rutting season, but the rut wasn't far enough along to put a rank taste in the meat. The deer packed a heavy layer of fat. Print preferred beef—as long as it wasn't Olive beef—but a plate of venison chops did have its appeal from time to time.

He tugged the heavy coat tighter over his chest, pulled his hat down against the freshening north wind and swung aboard the brown. Buckshot moved out in a smooth foxtrot at the touch of Print's heels. The sorrel followed, still snorting and dancing at the smell of blood. Print sniffed the north wind which whistled beneath the lowering clouds. He could smell the rain. It would be a cold rain, but it would refill the earth tanks the Olives and their hired hands had dug to trap the runoff. The rain also would replenish the springs that slaked the thirst of Olive cattle. All in all, he thought, a pretty nice day.

Print reined Buckshot north from the creek, following a cattle trail along a shallow draw which led in the general direction of home. He rode with ease, relaxed but alert to the sounds and smells of the country. The broken timber, brush, rolling hills, and the creeks and gullies eroded by the passing of time and wind and water provided any number of good spots for an ambush. Rumors were that Turk Turner and his neighbor, old man James Crow, had been doing some whiskey talking of late. Print didn't put much faith in rumors, but a careless man could miss out on a venison dinner. Maybe a hell of a lot more—

Print almost didn't hear the sound through the moan of the

wind. The soft nicker of a young horse was brief but unmistakable, and close by. There were no Olive riders in this area today.

Print pulled Buckshot to a stop and waited, testing the wind, and heard nothing. That didn't mean there was nothing out there. He slid his Henry from the saddle boot, hitched Buckshot and the pack horse to a pinoak and crabbed up the rocky side of a low ridge.

Moments later he saw a muted flicker of color fifty yards to his right. At the same time he heard a curse, muted by the wind, and the jangle of bits. The rider came into view at a bend of the ridge astride a big bay, leading a linebacked dun. The dun was an Olive horse. The horseman wasn't an Olive hand. He wore a heavy buffalo coat and his head was tilted down against the bite of the wind.

Print cocked the Henry and waited until the horseman was thirty paces away, then stepped into the trail. He swung the rifle to his shoulder, lined the sights on the horseman's chest and squeezed the trigger.

The Henry thumped against Print's shoulder. The man on the bay twisted sharply in the saddle and cried out as the rifle slug slammed into his body. He tumbled into the sandy trail as the startled bay jumped aside.

Print chambered a fresh round and waited. The bay ran a few yards and stopped, snorting nervously, the young dun still tied by a neckrope to the empty saddle. The downed man stirred and tried to sit up. He made it as far as one elbow before he noticed the bore of the Henry pointed at him. "Make one wrong move and the back of your head will be somewhere in Mexico," Print said.

The wounded man stopped moving.

"That's an Olive horse you were leading. Horse thieves don't live long on Olive land."

The man on the ground looked at Print, gray eyes showing the glaze of shock and pain. "You got a nasty chunk of lead in me," the wounded man said. "You going to kill me, go ahead and get it done."

Print's finger tightened on the trigger, then eased. "Man ought to know the name of the thief he's going to kill," Print said.

"Name's Murday. Rob Murday."

"You ride for Turk Turner?"

Murday nodded, then grimaced in pain. "A couple months." Murday's eyes regained some of their focus. He stared at Print. "You must be Print Olive."

"That's right."

"Jesus Christ. Just my luck. Pa always said I'd get killed someday. I didn't figure it so soon."

"Why'd you steal that horse, Murday?"

Murday managed a weak grin. "On account of it's a sight easier to steal 'em and sell 'em than to catch 'em and break 'em. Why the hell else would a man steal a horse?"

The anger suddenly drained from Print. He chuckled aloud. "I'll be double damned. I found something here I never thought I'd see—an honest thief." He studied Murday with care. The young man's face was weathered but mostly unlined, the eyes now alert and defiant despite the pain.

On an impulse Print lowered the hammer of the rifle and knelt beside the young thief. "At least you've got some sand. Maybe I won't kill you after all. How bad you hit?"

Murday lifted his heavy coat away from his right shoulder and studied the wound. "Not bad. Slug didn't hit a big blood vessel or I'd be dead by now, I reckon."

Print snorted in disgust. "This damn Henry hasn't got much more punch than a peashooter. Got to get me a real rifle one of these days. One that'll take a man in half. Let's have a look." He put the weapon on the ground and examined Murday's wound. "You'll live. Can you ride?"

Murday tried to stand. His legs wouldn't support him. "Hope to hell I can, 'cause I can't walk."

"You packing a handgun?"

"No."

Print ran a hand around Murday's belt and against his boots, then shook his head. "Piss-poor horse thief goes around without a sidearm," he said.

Murday lifted his undamaged shoulder in a half shrug. "Can't afford one. If I had any money I wouldn't be stealing horses."

Print squatted before Murday, rolled a cigarette and fired it with a lucifer scratched against a rock. "You look like a man who might know some cow."

"I speak it some."

"Well, if I don't kill you for a horse thief, you think you could work for me?"

Suspicion flashed in Murday's gray eyes. "Listen, Olive, if you're stringing me along before you kill me, just forget the bullshit and get on with it."

Print handed the cigarette to Murday and waited until he had inhaled a long drag. "I'm getting soft in my old age, Murday. I don't know why, but I like you. Instead of hanging you I think I'll take you home, patch you up and give you a job."

"Why?"

Print shrugged. "Damned if I know." He stood. "I'll catch your horse. We'll try to figure out later if I've lost my mind completely or just getting a little squirrelly. Or maybe trying to drive Turk Turner loco trying to figure why I didn't kill you."

FOUR

Olive Ranch
June 1869

Print Olive reined the young bay to a head-slinging stop at the crest of a low rise overlooking his new ranch headquarters. Behind the barn a half-dozen men worked at fitting trimmed logs into a large holding pen. The corral, almost as big as a lot of farms around Lawrence Chapel, was nearly complete. When it was finished Print's ranch would be in full operation.

And, he reminded himself with satisfaction, everything was moving along faster than he had expected.

The deal he had cut with Dudley Snyder and Fred Smith had paid off like a faro dealer on a bad night. Dudley and Fred had agreed to add Olive stock to the herd they trailed to railhead. The herd and its four hundred of Print's steers had been among the first to reach Abilene. The cattle were in better flesh than those which followed. Dudley had the edge with the buyers and he knew how to take advantage of it. After expenses and Dudley's commission Print had cleared better than eleven thousand dollars, about twenty-eight dollars a steer.

That money had financed payroll, ranch expenses, expansion of the ranch holdings by another section and completion of the new headquarters with a substantial sum left over in the Miller Brothers & Robertson Bank in Taylor.

Print Olive was on his way to becoming one of the richest men in Williamson County.

Print had chosen the site for his new home with care and supervised the building himself. The five-room main house was built on a base of sturdy hardwood logs with whitewashed planks topping off the structure.

Chimneys of native stone rose from the kitchen, living room and the larger bedroom. A shotgun-style bunkhouse made of logs and stone sat twenty paces beyond the main house. Cottonwoods, one huge oak and a couple of native pecan trees kept the grinding early summer sun at bay over the buildings. A new windmill clunked and creaked in the light breeze. It pumped sweet, clear water into a massive cedar holding tank. The mill supplied both the living quarters and the wooden watering troughs for livestock at the barn.

In a small round corral at the side of the barn Print saw Jim Kelly topping out a new horse. The animal was pitching and squealing, but Kelly sat solid in the saddle. This one, Print thought, would be no contest. Jim had things well under control.

Several times during the past couple of months Print allowed himself the pleasure of stopping on the hill to survey his growing domain. He always felt a surge of pride in the place, although he would go to great lengths to hide that feeling from anyone riding with him.

He knew Louise had no such reservations. She loved her new house and seldom missed a chance to describe its wonders to the ladies in her Methodist church circle—or any other woman who would listen. Print understood her feelings. It was the first place Louise had ever lived that she could call her own home. And she had driven even deeper roots into the place since the birth of the baby.

Print Olive was proud of his son. But, as with the ranch, he went out of his way to hide his pride. Cooing and cuddling was woman's trade. It was a sign of weakness in a man in Print's eyes.

William Olive, already known simply as Billy, was almost a year old. He had his father's robust build and temper. Without the help of Anna Maria Ontiveros, young Billy and the responsibilities of running a home would have been too much for Louise. Anna Maria was an expert at such things. She had seven children of her own.

Billy's birth had changed Louise physically, broadening her hips, adding a bit of flesh to her waist and filling out her breasts. Print liked the changes. Louise seemed less frail now. He liked her new attitude toward life even more. She seldom complained, almost never whined or nagged about this or that, and there was a light in her eyes that hadn't been there before. Strange, Print thought, how a nest and a nestling could change a woman.

Print was as near to content as he had been in years. Cattle prices were still heading up and the Olive herds were growing fast. Ira, Jay and Marion had their own places, their own brands, and the brothers shared the open range Print had claimed. Print's own herd now was pushing five thousand head. Ira had a thousand or so, Jay nearly that many, and about five hundred wore Marion's brand, mostly for the convenience of the other brothers. Marion had little interest in cattle, so he had turned use of his land over to his brothers. Marion, Print thought with a touch of disgust, always had run a bit to the lace-drawers side. He preferred a store clerk's apron to the saddle. At least when he was running Jim Olive's mercantile business, Marion wasn't in the way around a herd.

The young bay between Print's knees snorted and stamped its front feet, anxious to get back to water and feed. Print was about to drive a spur into the bay to teach him some manners when he spotted the rider. The horseman was in a hurry, headed for the Olive place at a fast lope. Print watched until he could identify the rider, then spurred the bay into motion. Something had Ira's dander up, the way he was pushing that horse.

Print was waiting at the hitch rail when Ira pulled his lathered gray to a stop. Ira's thick brows were bunched, his jaw squared, and his big hands trembled in fury against the reins.

"Some sonofabitch out there needs hanging, Print," Ira said by way of greeting. It had to be bad, Print thought, to push Ira to the cussing stage.

"What happened?"

"Somebody killed three of our best cows this morning. Shot 'em. And hamstrung that good brindle bull of ours."

Print barked a sharp curse. "Where?"

"Tonkawa Flat. A good two miles inside our land lease."

"Hide men?"

"No. Didn't skin 'em. Just killed the cows and left them lay. The bull's down, hocked clear through."

Fury balled a growing fist in Print's gut. Killing a man's cows for no reason was bad enough. Cutting the rear hock tendon on a prize bull crippled the animal, left it unable to move and in agony. It was a mindless and brutal act beyond Print's comprehension.

Print shucked his Henry from his saddle boot and checked the loads. "You'll need a fresh horse, Ira. Me, too. This bay's too green to be around any shooting." He yelled for Rob Murday. "Catch that blaze-faced sorrel for Ira," he told him. "I'll need Buckshot. Tell Jim Kelly to forget the broncs. We need him and that Dragoon of his. Hurry it up, Rob!"

Fifteen minutes later the three men rode out, headed toward Tonkawa Flat at a fast trot. "Any tracks, Ira?" Print asked over the thud of hooves and creak of saddle leather.

"A few. Looked like three shod horses. Didn't recognize any of the hoofprints. Headed north."

"If they can be followed, Jim can find them," Print said. "The bastards won't get any mercy from this outfit."

They reached Tonkawa Flat after an hour's ride. Print's rage flared higher as he spotted the buzzards circling overhead. A few minutes later he sat astride Buckshot, looking down at three longhorn carcasses. The birds had already been at them, but Print could see the obvious bullet holes in the animals' foreheads.

Fifty yards away the bull lay on its side in a wild plum thicket along a shallow draw. The animal raised its head and bawled fitfully. The bull's right hind leg flopped out of control. Blood still flowed from the deep cut that had severed the tendon above the hock. Print raised his rifle and shot the bull between the eyes. There was nothing else he could do. The animal's head flopped, eyes glazing as its legs twitched in death throes.

"The dirty bastard who did this is going to pay," Print muttered through clenched teeth as he levered a fresh round into the chamber of the Henry.

Jim Kelly picked up the trail within minutes. For three hours they followed. Print's need for blood boiled hotter by the minute. Then the tracks intersected the heavily traveled road leading to Taylor and vanished amid half a hundred other hoofprints and wagon wheel marks.

Kelly shook his head. "Sorry, boss. There ain't no way I can pick 'em out from here in. Could have gone any which way. North to Taylor, west to Round Rock, anywhere. Nothin' special about the prints, either. I couldn't pick 'em out if they was standin' in front of me right now."

Print's shoulders sagged in frustration, the unrelieved fury churning his gut.

"What now, Print?"

"What I'd like to do, Ira," Print said, "is ride into Taylor and shoot the place up until somebody points us to who did this. But that wouldn't solve a thing." He fell silent for a moment, trying to think. "Ira, ride on into town. If I go in there myself I might kill somebody, the way I feel right now. Let the word out that Print Olive will pay a hundred dollars cash money to anybody who can tell me who's responsible for killing those cattle. While you're at it, pass the word that anybody trespassing on Olive land will be considered a thief and shot on the spot."

He scratched a thumbnail across the stubble of beard on his chin. "Jim and I will head on back to the ranch. I want to set up some way we can keep scouts out on the range. Like in army patrols. Maybe catch them in the act if they're stupid enough to try something like this again. Then, I'm calling a family war council at Pa's house."

Print Olive leaned back in his chair at his father's long dining room table and waited impatiently for the start of the family meeting. Such sessions once were a weekly thing in Jim Olive's house. In the early days the sessions were as much a recitation of the sins of the sons as a hard look at serious family matters. Print had taken his share of verbal trips to the woodpile at this table.

Now things had changed. The Olives held such councils only in times of crisis or when a major decision on the family's future and fortunes had to be made.

Jim Olive still kept his seat at the head of the table, but everyone in the room knew that the power of leadership had passed from father to son. Print, seated at Jim Olive's left, served as organizer, planner, accountant and manager of the beef operation, which had long since outstripped Jim Olive's farming and mercantile business in importance.

As he waited, Print studied the faces of the men at the table. Ira sat across from Print; at Ira's right, Jay; across from Jay at Print's left, Marion; and in the fifth chair, Bob, youngest of the

Olive boys. Except for the physical similarity to their mother, Print thought, the brothers were as different as men could be.

Ira was the quiet one, clean-shaven, slow to anger. Ira's solid, muscular body was erect in his chair, his dark brown eyes flicking about the room. Ira seldom spoke except to answer a question or raise a point of some magnitude. Beneath the calm surface, however, lay a toughness that few men dared challenge. Print recalled that when they were boys Ira had tried twice to whip Print in barnyard brawls before giving up the idea. He'd come closer to pulling it off than he suspected. Print had been more than somewhat relieved when Ira decided to drop that project.

Jay was tall and angular, wiry, with a narrow face just beginning to develop lines from the wind and sun. He was a good hand with young horses. Jay was the Olive brother most popular with the hired hands, laughing and joking with them as they worked. He wasn't afraid to get himself scraped and muddied pulling a steer out of a bog when he could just as easily tell someone else to do it. All the Olive boys had a middling fair education, but Jay was the one found most often with his nose in a book. He was also the most cautious of the Olives. Jay thought things through before he acted. Print hoped it didn't get him in trouble one day.

Marion Olive was the father's favorite. Marion had his mother's coloration and his father's ambition—which was to say, not much. He didn't drink, smoke, get into fights or even swear. Consequently, Print didn't pay much attention to Marion or his opinions.

If any two of them were alike, Print thought, it would be himself and the youngest brother. Bob was a few months shy of fourteen, tall for his age, his body just beginning to muscle out. His hands were almost as big as Print's own. And he shared Print's temper. The boy was a real heller, a mirror image of Print at that age. Bob already carried the scars of a dozen fist fights, usually with older and bigger boys. Impulsive and reckless, he had already broken an arm and a leg. Jim Olive had groused on occasion that a man couldn't get a decent nap around the house for the sound of snapping bones. Bob had only recently earned a spot at the family table, except for when he was in trouble with Jim Olive, which was so often he had practically been a fixture at the conferences most of his life. Bob had the makings of a good hand with horses and cattle. At times he could be stubborn and sullen, but Print could never stay angry with him for long. Print envied Bob's youthful exuberance. Being a kid was something Print felt, deep inside, that he had missed out on.

There was little idle chatter at Olive family business gatherings. The men sat and waited until Julia appeared, poured the ritual coffee, set the pot on warming bricks at Jim's right hand and quietly left to tend to other chores and leave the dining room clear for "man talk." As Julia retreated through the kitchen door Print heard Louise laugh at something the baby had done.

Jim Olive sipped at his coffee and cleared his throat, the signal for the meeting to begin.

"Print?"

Print grunted in disgust. "Our cow-killers are still out there somewhere. I thought it might be Turk Turner, but he was in Huntsville when we lost the stock. Went with old man Crow to bring that no-account son of Crow's home from the state pen. Ira's maybe turned up something."

"I don't put a whole lot of stock in it yet," Ira said solemnly. "I've still got some checking to do. But a drunk teamster over in Taylor nibbled at the reward bait just a bit. Said there was a new man down in Lee County, just off the southeast edge of our place. Settler name of Phreme. Deets Phreme. Also goes by D. R. Frame and a couple other names. This teamster says Phreme and two friends of his, maybe hired hands, rode in from the south the day our cows were killed. Said Phreme's knife sheath —he carries a blade like a Bowie—had fresh blood on it. Could be he hocked our bull, maybe not."

"He's worth checking up on, Pa," Print said. "Nobody I've talked to knows much about Phreme except that he fancies himself some kind of hardcase. I've asked Dudley Snyder to see what he can find out about him."

"That's all we have to go on?"

"That's it, Pa. None of our scouts have cut sign of anybody on our range. Our cattle haven't been bothered since the killings."

"Well, there's not much we can do about it now, I guess," Jim Olive said with a shrug. "We sure can't haul this Phreme fellow before the law without any proof. Besides, we can stand the loss of three cows and a bull easier than we can stand any more trouble."

Print's anger flared anew at his father's offhanded dismissal of the stock loss. "Dammit, Pa, it's not just four head of cattle we're talking about!" Print snapped. "If we let whoever did this get away with it we might as well just throw Olive range open to anybody who wants it!"

"Settle down, Print. I just said we can stand the loss, and there isn't anything we can do about it. So for now, the question is closed." Jim picked up his coffee cup and stared over the rim at Print. "Except for the trouble at the Flat, how does everything else look?"

Print forced himself to relax his clenched jaw, to control the urge to push the point. *If he won't help, by God, I'll just take care of it myself,* he thought. He sighed. "Not bad, Pa. Cattle prices are still going up. Dudley says he thinks they'll hit thirty to forty dollars a head a year from now. I've been thinking we should put our own herd together and point them north in a few months." Print's lips lifted in a tight, mirthless smile. "Looks like we're finally going to get back some of the money the damn Yankees did us out of. We've got hold of the reins, now that the Yanks are developing a taste for Texas beef."

"The war's over, Print," Jim Olive said. Before Print could reply, Jim said, "Any other family business to be discussed?"

"Yes, Pa," Bob said. "I want my own gun."

Jim Olive stared at Bob for a moment, then shook his head. "There's enough guns in this family now, and they're likely to bring us nothing but grief. You're just a boy—"

"Dammit, Pa, I'm near fourteen!" Bob's dark eyes glared in anger and defiance. "I'm man enough to carry a gun. I've done my share of the work around here. I'm not Little Brother anymore, in case you hadn't noticed."

"Mind your tone, young man!" Jim Olive's voice was sharp. "You'll not curse in this house!"

"Print does!"

"Print does a lot of things I don't approve of," Jim said. "That doesn't give *you* the right to do them."

Bob fell silent and glowered at his father, his thin lips clenched in a tight frown. The strained silence held at the table for a few moments, broken only by the steady tick of the mantel clock on its shelf.

"Pa," Print said at length, "Bob's got a point. When I was his age I had been packing a sidearm for over a year. Bob's out on the range as much as the rest of us. He's making a good enough hand that I can send him out alone now. What if he rides up on a lobo wolf or a coyote pack? Or what if he had happened onto whoever killed our cows while they were doing it? They'd likely have shot him along with the cows. He wouldn't have had a chance without a gun."

Bob glanced at Print, obviously pleased with the support, then back at his father. Jim Olive's face was drawn into a frown. "I just don't like the idea of a boy—"

"Do you like the idea of bringing him home face down across the saddle?" Print interrupted.

Jim Olive sat in silence for several heartbeats, then sighed heavily. "All right. I suppose you make sense, Print. These are dangerous times. But he needs to know how to use one if he carries it, so he doesn't shoot himself."

"Pa," Bob said, exasperated, "I know how to shoot—"

"No you don't, little brother," Print said. "You've fired my old Navy thirty-six a few times and my Remington once or twice. Knowing how to pull a trigger doesn't mean you know how to shoot. There's a difference. It's a difference you have to learn."

Bob opened his mouth to protest, apparently decided it was best not to antagonize his only backer, and fell silent.

"You can use my old Navy," Print said. "Jim Kelly can teach you how to handle a sidearm. There's not a better hand with a gun on this ranch, including me."

Bob suddenly grinned, realizing his older brother had flanked his father on the issue. He was going to get his handgun. "When do we start, Print?"

"Might as well start today. No Olive worth his salt dallies around once a decision's been made."

A knock on the door put a halt to the discussion. Rob Murday stepped into the room. "Sorry to interrupt, folks. There's a rider out here to see Print."

Print shoved his chair back and stood. "Pa?"

Jim Olive sighed. "I guess that's all for now."

Print strode to the door, stepped out into the sunlight and let a grin spread over his face. Deacon Scruggs sat astride a rail-thin, slab-sided bay gelding. Deacon still wore his battered Confederate campaign cap, its Third Arkansas insignia almost weathered away. A jagged scar ran from above his left eyebrow to his cheekbone. The eye was clouded, with no pupil visible. An ancient Springfield carbine dangled from a thong at the side of a worn cavalry saddle, and Scruggs had a bulky LeMat revolver tucked into his waistband.

"Well, I'll be damned," Print said. "Deacon, I figured you'd still be pushing a plow in that rockpile called Arkansas. Get down, before that bone bag you're riding falls over on you."

Scruggs stepped from the saddle, took Print's hand in a firm grip and grinned back at his old army friend. "You're lookin' good, Print," he said. "Heard you were doin' right well for yourself."

"Well enough for now, Deacon." Print draped an arm over Scrugg's thick shoulders. It was about as close as he ever came to an outright show of affection for another man. "What brings you down this way?"

"Little woman trouble up in Pine Bluff," Scruggs said. "Had to shoot a man took offense at the way I was treatin' his sister. The man was my brother-in-law."

"The woman?"

"Took after me with a double-bit axe when I shot her brother just before he would have lowered a shotgun hammer on me. Never liked her all that much, but by all that's holy I swear I never laid a hand on the wench. Last I saw of her she was wavin' that axe about a foot behind my horse's butt."

Print chuckled. "I can believe it, Deacon. You always did have a way with the ladies. Come in, meet the family."

Print steered Deacon Scruggs inside and made the introductions. Bob seemed a bit surly with his greeting, but Print knew it wasn't for dislike of the man. Scruggs's arrival was merely an unwelcome delay in Bob's getting his hands on a pistol. Print understood the youth's eagerness and lack of patience. He'd been the same way at that age.

"Deacon was with the Third Arkansas when it was part of Hood's Brigade," Print said as he poured a cup of coffee for Deacon. "We went through Gettysburg and the Wilderness and points between together, then shared cooties in a Yank prison camp. I guess you could say he's the closest friend I've got outside the family. Ugliest nurse a man could have, but one of the best."

Later, after the rest of the family drifted away to tend chores, Deacon and Print sat at the table swapping war stories and taking turns cursing the United States Army, carpetbaggers, politicians and other assorted Northern types. Finally, Deacon leaned forward, his heavy shoulders hunched.

"Print," he said, "I heard you were gettin' to be somethin' of a stud hoss down here in Texas. I didn't realize how much of a hoss until I got here and started askin' around. Got sort of unfriendly, some places I asked. Anyway, I was hopin' you'd know of somebody needs a hand. I got fifty cents in my pocket, a dirt farm back in Arkansas I can't sell and maybe a sheriff lookin' for me to boot. I need a place where nobody knows me, and I need work."

"You got it, Deacon. I can use another man. I supply the horses and gear. Looks like you can use some of each. I know you can handle guns. Can you handle cattle?"

"I ain't too old to learn."

"It's settled, then. You'll work with my crew. Pay's thirty a month and all you can eat. Speaking of which, are you hungry?"

Deacon shrugged and grinned. "Shouldn't be. Hell, I ate half a biscuit and a piece of sowbelly. Day before yesterday, I think it was."

"I'll ask Ma to rustle up something," Print said, heading for the kitchen. Bob intercepted him at the doorway.

"How about my gun?" Bob asked.

Print cuffed him lightly on the shoulder. "Soon, Bob. That Navy's not going to walk off in the next hour or so." He gestured toward the front door. "Take care of Deacon's horse. Give him an extra bait of grain. Poor animal looks like he hasn't seen corn or oats since Arkansas. Put the spare stock saddle on Pa's bay for Deacon. Soon as we get them both fed we'll ride over to my place and get you that gun."

FIVE

Olive Ranch
July 1869

Louise Olive swiped at a sweat-slicked lock of hair plastered to her forehead and tried to comfort the squalling baby in her arms.

Little Billy Olive wasn't taking kindly to her attempts to wean him from the breast. The boy had a temper, a yowl loud enough to wake the dead, and he wasn't shy about letting his displeasure be known. But all the yelling in the world wasn't going to change the fact that William was almost a year and a half old—or the fact that Louise's milk was drying up. Neither of them really had a choice in the matter. It was weaning time or starving time.

She wedged a spoon of mashed peas into the child's mouth. It immediately sprayed back in her face. She grimaced, wiped her lips with the sleeve of her dress and dipped another spoon of greenish goo.

"William Olive," she said, slightly vexed, "you and your father are kernels off the same ear of corn. I never met two more stubborn men in my life. Maybe I can't do anything about him, but I'm bigger than you are and you're going to eat these peas if we stay here all afternoon."

The peas came back at her again.

"*Señora, por favor.*"

Louise squinted through a greenish haze as Anna Maria Ontiveros strode into the room, her wide hips almost brushing the narrow doorway, a gentle smile on her placid face. She held a saucer in a hand surprisingly small for her bulk. "I have brought some sweet potatoes. Perhaps the young one just does not like peas."

Billy's yowling stopped abruptly. The plump face smoothed from its contortions of anger and dissolved into a hiccuping grin as Anna Maria leaned forward to smile at him. The Mexican woman touched a clean spoon to the pulverized orange mass in the saucer and raised it to Billy's lips. The child's tongue sampled the sweet potatoes. He opened his mouth wide, accepted the food, drooled a trace of orange over his chin and popped his mouth open again.

"There," Anna Maria said, handing the saucer to Louise. "He will eat now, I think."

Louise smiled in gratitude at her combination cook, house-keeper and companion. "Anna Maria, you are a godsend," she said. "You always seem to know what to do."

Anna Maria shrugged her broad shoulders. "It is a simple matter," she said. "A woman gives her man what he wants, whether the man is little like this one or big like Señor Print. A man is a man no matter his size." She waited until Louise had gotten two spoons of sweet potatoes into her now happy offspring, then turned and left the room.

Louise settled into the routine of feeding her son. Except for the minor skirmishes with Billy, her life was better than she had any right to expect, she thought. She had money, nice clothes, a new buggy for her Sunday trips to the Methodist church at Lawrence Chapel and plenty of food now. But she still remembered the pain of an empty belly, the humiliation of wearing clothes that were little more than rags, of sitting alone while the other schoolchildren ate their bacon and biscuits or whatever they had brought for lunch. She sat alone because she had no lunch.

The hard labor of her childhood and young adult years remained fresh in her mind. Washing, cooking when there was something to cook, tending livestock, mending and darning, being constantly at her grandfather's call when he had one of his "spells" that only the corked white jug seemed to cure. All those were past but not forgotten. Others now did the labor. Louise's calluses had softened. She had everything a woman could want.

Except contentment.

The whispered gossip overheard at church services and socials stung Louise Olive.

". . . disappeared, left that poor woman alone and destitute with four children . . ." A cursory glance in Louise's direction.

". . . you ask me, it was Print Olive done it . . ." A condescending sniff. ". . . you'd think those Olives had enough already, without terrorizing poor folks who just want to make a living . . ."

Another sideward glance, a hand raised alongside a mouth. ". . . four families run off this month . . . feel sorry for Louise, living with that man . . . no good will come of him, the Lord'll see to that . . ."

At first Louise dismissed the mutterings as simple jealousy. Then, gradually, she began to notice things that had escaped her before. Print would make some remark about a certain settler moving in on "Olive range," and the settler would be gone within a week. Twice she had seen whole families pass through Lawrence Chapel, their few possessions piled on a creaky wagon pulled by a gaunt mule. Another time the scene was the same except the woman was alone on the wagon seat. Sunlight glistened from tears on her face. And the Olive Ranch herd and grazing lands expanded by the day, it seemed.

There were almost a dozen hired hands in the bunkhouse now. Most of them were hard-eyed men who carried guns at all times, even to the outhouse. Print had hired a cook for the men and an aging Mexican to care for the stock.

A retching sound broke into her reverie. Billy's face twisted in a grimace. A small pink tongue pushed the last spoon of sweet potatoes from his mouth onto the stained bib across his chest. He swiped a chubby hand through the orange-green mess, smeared the goo into a handful of Louise's hair and whimpered. She set the spoon and saucer aside and hoisted the baby onto a shoulder, patting his back with her free hand. The whimpering slowly subsided.

Louise's thoughts drifted back to Print as she gently rocked the child. Print seemed more distant now. He seldom touched her except when he felt the need for her body. He almost never laughed, but he had never been much for laughter. Despite the rapid growth of his ranch and his fortune he seemed more driven than ever. He was in the saddle from dawn until dark. And he spent most of his few spare hours in Taylor, Round Rock or Georgetown, drinking and gambling. It was as if, she thought, Print Olive was a man possessed—cursed by one of the old hags suspected of witchcraft in the East Texas hills.

Louise wanted to cry out to Print, to tell him they had enough, more than any family would need. She didn't dare. Anna Maria was right. It wasn't a woman's place to tell her man how to run his business. She knew she should be satisfied that she had a solid roof over her head, plenty to eat and a son—albeit a somewhat messy one—to absorb the leftover love she longed to give her husband.

The baby's breathing against her shoulder deepened into sleep. A few more minutes and she could put the child in his small mail-order bed. Then she would slip into a tub and try to soak away her concern in luxury.

The child started as the whipcrack of a gunshot tore through the open window, followed rapidly by four more. Billy's first startled cry had reached a full rolling boil of screaming outrage and fear by the time the echoes of the gunshots stopped.

"Shush, Billy," Louise soothed, stroking the boy's back. "It's just your Uncle Bob playing with his gun."

A flush of aggravation swept Louise. Every free moment of Bob Olive's time seemed to be covered in powder smoke. He practiced endlessly with that old Navy revolver under the watchful eye of Nigger Jim Kelly.

Louise Olive didn't dare mention it to any of the men in her family, but deep inside she hated guns. She hated the noise, the smoke, the death and destruction, the scars they left in shattered flesh. She resented the time men devoted to them, cleaning, oiling, caressing them as if the guns were mistresses. If Print spent half the time with her that he spent with his guns, she would be a happy woman.

She clutched the baby against her shoulder and tried to soothe the child. "Billy," she whispered, "I pray you'll never need to own a gun—" She glanced toward the window as another volley of gunfire sounded and shook her head in disgust and sadness. *That gun will be the death of you, Bob Olive,* she thought, *and I just hope it doesn't drag the rest of this family down with you . . .*

• • • •

Print pulled his horse to a stop at the top of a low rise overlooking the southern range of the Olive holdings. He raised a hand.

At his side, Ira Olive and Deacon Scruggs reined in their mounts. A quarter mile away two riders lazed along, headed north.

"That the Turner and Crow fellows you been growlin' about, Print?" Deacon asked.

"No. That's Deets Phreme and one of his saddle tramp friends." Print pulled his Henry from its saddle boot. "Grab some steel, boys. I've been wanting to talk to that bastard."

Fifteen minutes later Deets Phreme reined his horse around a scrub oak clump and found himself looking down the bore of Print Olive's rifle. Phreme barked a startled curse, started to reach for the handgun at his belt and as quickly decided against it. At Print Olive's left, Ira held a rifle; at his right, another Olive rider pointed a wicked-looking LeMat pistol at Phreme's left eye. Phreme's Mexican companion abruptly checked his mount and raised his hands to shoulder level, eyes wide in fear.

"What the hell do you think you're doing on Olive land, Phreme?" Print's tone was cold and deadly. "Come back to kill more of my cows?"

Phreme's gaze shifted from one Olive rider to another, then back to Print. "I don't know what you're talking about, Olive," he said. "Jorge and I were just tracking some of our stock that drifted up this way."

"In a pig's ass you were, Phreme. You were looking for Olive stock. You plan to cripple another bull for me?" The venom in Print Olive's voice cut through Phreme's initial surprise at the sudden appearance of the three horsemen.

"Olive, I don't know one damn thing about any dead cows or crippled bulls. I got as much right to hunt my own strays here as any man."

"That's right, Phreme. You got as much right as any other man. Which is to say, no right at all." Print waved the muzzle of the Henry almost under Phreme's nose. The Mexican began to babble in Spanish, too rapidly for Print to follow. Print didn't care. It was Phreme he wanted. "Shuck those gunbelts. Slow and easy."

Deets Phreme fought back the urge to draw his weapon. He

knew he would be dead before his pistol cleared leather. Growing fear pushed against his bladder. He unbuckled his holster and let the belt and pistol drop into the dirt. He heard a thump behind him and knew Jorge had done the same.

"Step down and move away from the guns."

Phreme and Jorge did as they were told. Phreme felt the clutch of an icy fist in his gut as Print Olive sheathed his rifle and reached for a lariat tied to his saddle. Phreme had less fear of a bullet than he had of a noose.

"What are you going to do, Olive? You can't hang a man for hunting his own cattle. We got laws—"

"There's only one law here, Phreme. Olive law." Print swung from the saddle, rope in hand. Jorge fell to his knees at the sight of the lariat, praying and pleading in Spanish. "I'm not going to hang you, Phreme," Print said. "God knows I should, but I won't." He shook out a loop, then folded the honda back against his wrist. Three feet of doubled Manila hemp dangled from his fist. "When I get through with you, Phreme, you'll think twice before you hamstring my stock again."

The doubled rope whistled forward and slammed into Phreme's cheek. The hemp stripped a layer of skin from his face and sent his hat flying. Print whipped the rope back across Phreme's face; Phreme tried to grab the lariat, missed, and a third time the coarse rope drew blood. Phreme's vision blurred as the hemp ripped the bridge of his nose. He staggered and went to his knees.

Print swung the rope again and again. There was no escape for Phreme. The lariat raked his face and chest. When he tried to turn aside the hemp tore across his shoulders and back.

"That's enough, Print," Ira finally said. "He should have learned his lesson by now."

Ira's voice seemed to calm the demon in Print. He stared at the man writhing on the ground as he re-coiled the rope. Crimson seeped from welts across Phreme's face and torso. One ear, partly torn from his head, dribbled a steady trickle of blood. Phreme's shirt was in tatters, the marks of the hemp lash bright against pale skin.

The Mexican continued to beg, holding his hands out as if to ward off a similar beating. "Shut up, Jorge," Print snapped in Spanish.

Jorge shut up.

Print picked up the dropped gunbelts and looped them over his saddle horn. He pulled Phreme's rifle from the scabbard and slammed the weapon against a nearby rock. The impact bent the barrel at a sharp angle. Print reversed his grip, shattered the stock against the stone and tossed the useless weapon at the moaning man's feet.

"Consider yourself lucky this time, Phreme," Print said. "If I ever find you on Olive land again, I'll gut you and hang you with your own intestines. If you've got any sense at all you'll clear out of this country and stay out. You hear me?"

Deets Phreme raised his battered head and glared at Print as best he could through eyes almost swollen shut. "You—bastard." His words were slurred through torn and bloody lips. "You ain't heard the last of me, Olive. I'll kill you for this."

"Anytime you feel stud hoss enough, Phreme, I'll be around." Print abruptly stood, retrieved the reins and mounted his gelding. "Let's go," he said. "We've stomped enough rattlers for one day."

The three men rode in silence for the better part of a mile. Deacon glanced at Ira. The man's face was pale beneath the weathered tan. The brutal beating seemed to have shaken Ira more than a killing would have. Print seemed relaxed. He rode loose in the saddle, the fires of fury gone from the dark eyes.

"Print," Deacon said, "you may've made a mistake back there. Maybe you should've just shot the bastard and saved yourself some trouble down the road."

The faintest hint of a smile touched Print's face. "Maybe. Maybe not. I think he'll get the idea he's not welcome around here and move on. Others have got the notion to travel from a lot less."

"I doubt it, Print," Ira broke in. "Deets Phreme looks a little tougher than the average homesteader. Somewhat like you, maybe. A stubborn man with pride. I think you'd best watch your back. Maybe we all better."

Print snorted in disgust.

"Well, my friend," Deacon said, "remember what Captain Jenkins yammered at us from day one of that little war. 'Never underestimate the enemy.' " Deacon pulled a tobacco twist from his pocket, gnawed off a sizable hunk and tucked it into a cheek. "I don't think that Phreme fellow's goin' to take kindly to bein' whipped like an ugly stepsister."

Print twisted in the saddle to scowl at his friend. "Deacon, you're a good man to ride with. But you can sure enough talk a badger plumb out of its hole. Let's see if we can't get some ranch work done now that the fun's over."

SIX

Round Rock
March 1870

Deacon Scruggs wasn't highly educated, but it didn't take much book smart for a man to figure out he had ridden into the makings of a range war.

He leaned against the Emporium's stained pine bar, nursing a mug of lukewarm beer and killing time until the gunsmith two doors down finished fixing the old LeMat.

Deacon listened with half an ear to bits and pieces of conversation in the watering hole. The place was crowded, but not to the point of discomfort. Deacon wasn't so sure about the rest of Williamson County.

In the fourteen months since he had signed on with Print Olive, settlers had been pouring into the county until it was nearly as crowded as Arkansas. And all the settlers wanted land. Deacon could understand why. Williamson County had a lot to offer. Clean, sweet water, plenty of timber for building, good grass for livestock and a variety of fertile soils that would help a man grow nearly anything he wanted. If he hadn't already spent more than his share of time looking at the ass end of a mule, Deacon mused, he wouldn't mind having a share of farmland around here himself.

The settlers came full of hopes and dreams. Some came with bogus land titles sold by carpetbaggers and thieving promoters. Instead of a quarter section and a good life in the land of milk and honey, a lot of them wound up caught between two factions. On the one side were the established ranchers like the Olives and their friends, the Snyder brothers and Fred Smith. On the other side were the smaller farmers and ranchers. Neither side was likely to give up land through any Christian generosity toward strangers.

Some other big ranchers who had made their start in East or Central Texas had pulled out under the crush of settlers. Richard King went south, claimed a big chunk of land and kept right on growing until he owned most of the Gulf Coast plains outright. Shanghai Pierce had moved south and west and tripled his range within a year.

Print Olive had no intention of going anywhere.

Deacon could see the range war building, and building fast. But he couldn't pin down just who the enemy was.

Rumors picked up here and there and considerable bunkhouse gossip hadn't narrowed the field much. Print Olive had made too many enemies to pick from. Any one of the farmers or ranchers who wanted Olive land—or had been pushed from it—could be behind the rumors and whispered accusations leveled against the Olives. Deacon was reasonably sure in his own mind that Turk Turner and James Crow led, or at least agitated, one faction against them. Then there was Deets Phreme. The young settler had not forgotten the whipping at Print's hands. He hadn't fled the country as Print had expected. To Deacon, Deets Phreme was a live coal on top of a powder wagon. It was only a matter of time until he burned through and exploded.

Deacon decided it boiled down to the Olives and a handful of other big landowners against the rest of the county. Deacon was no military genius where tactics were concerned, but he did know one thing. You had to know who an enemy was before you could fight him. Another thing was for damn sure. Print Olive would fight.

He had known Print almost as long as anyone outside the family, but he still didn't really understand the man. Nobody who knew Print could question his guts; he seemed to have no fear in him. Many a time Print Olive had been the first man in the charge against a Yank stronghold. It was as if he believed he was beyond killing. Deacon had grown tired of the slaughter. The taking of every Yankee life seemed to rest more heavily on his shoulders.

Print Olive had thrived on the killing.

It had been a legend turned accepted fact in the First Texas and beyond that Print Olive never laughed unless he had just killed a man. Deacon Scruggs knew that wasn't completely true. He had heard Print chuckle aloud after just breaking an arm or leg once in a while. It seemed like when the Maker built Print, He left out something. Compassion, maybe, or a conscience. But He had put in a cold capacity for violence. The resulting work was one very dangerous man.

Deacon sipped at the beer. It left a bitter taste on the back of his tongue. He wondered what had left such a taste in Print's mouth. It seemed the man had everything he could possibly want—a growing ranch, fine house, a pretty wife and a healthy young son. He had asked Print about it once, and near got his head bit off for his troubles. "Dammit, Deacon," Print had growled, "no man, not even a friend, is going to tell me when I've got enough." Deacon decided it might be in his best interest not to pursue that line of questioning further.

Something else about Print seemed a little off-center, like a wobbly wheel on a new buggy. His wife was afraid of him. Deacon could see it in her eyes, in the way she kind of moved around on tiptoe when he was in the house. That just didn't seem right. A woman shouldn't be afraid of her man. And Print never messed with the baby the way a real daddy should. Deacon sensed Print was proud of the boy, even if little Billy was hell on short wheels most of the time. But Print just sort of left the boy alone. Like he did Louise.

The idea came slowly and a little embarrassingly to Deacon Scruggs. It wasn't the sort of thing a man thought about, much less mentioned out loud. But he had an idea that maybe Print Olive had never learned how to love.

Deacon finished his beer and forced the thought from his mind. Whatever was eating at Print didn't change the fact that he was a friend. Or that Print Olive and Deacon Scruggs had pulled each other's fat out of the fire more than once. Deacon Scruggs had never turned his back on a friend. When the shooting started, he wouldn't this time, either. Print's other hands felt the same way. It was loyalty to a brand as much as to a man. Print worked a man hard but mostly treated him right no matter his color. Print had a dozen men on his payroll now, not counting family, and two thirds of them were either Mexican or Negro.

Deacon grinned to himself, remembering the day he'd asked Print about the crew. Deacon mentioned that it seemed strange a dedicated Confederate like Print hired Negroes, and everybody knew Texans hated Mexicans worse than a toothache. The answer had been simple and to the point. "They work just as hard as white men," Print said, "but they work cheaper and bitch less."

The grin faded in a flare of irritation as Deacon felt a finger poke the back of his shoulder. He turned to face a beefy, blond man clad in worn coveralls and down-at-heel brogans. The farmer's face was flushed from the effects of cheap whiskey.

"You one of them Olive hands?" The farmer punctuated the question with another poke at Deacon's shoulder.

"I ride for Print Olive. And if you like that damn finger, keep it off me."

The farmer's hand dropped to his side. "Give Olive a message," he said, his words heavy with anger. "He's done run off his last settler around here. He ain't gonna be the stud rooster in this henhouse much longer."

Deacon sighed. He stared at the farmer and wondered if this was going to wind up in a brawl. The farmer could be a hard man to take. He stood just under six foot tall and packed about two hundred thirty pounds, most of it muscle from wrestling stumps and pushing a plow.

"I reckon," Deacon said softly, "that if you're going to be the one takes Print Olive down, you ought to be the one tells him. I'm a hired hand, not a messenger boy. You got a beef with Print, tell him to his face."

The farmer's lips pulled back in a semblance of a sneer. "It ain't just me. Half the county's fed up with Olive lordin' it over 'em. He's smart, he'll pull in his horns before somebody knocks 'em off."

The big man spun on a heel and stalked away a bit unsteadily.

Deacon let him go. The man hadn't said anything Deacon hadn't heard before. He realized he might be missing a chance to get some names, but it sounded like the farmer was making whiskey-talk. He'd mention it to Print, at any rate.

A few minutes later Deacon stepped into the warm wash of spring sun, snorted the stale smoke and whiskey scent of the Emporium from his nostrils and made his way to the gunsmith's shop.

The gunsmith, a wizened little man who could have been anywhere from forty to seventy, looked up from his workbench as Deacon stepped inside. The old man smiled and nodded. "Gun's ready. First time I worked on a LeMat since the fish et Jonah." He reached under the counter and hefted the holstered weapon. "Afraid I'll have to charge you two bucks, mister," he said. "Lot of money, but I had to file up a new barrel selector."

Deacon eased the LeMat from its holster and examined the smith's work. The LeMat was ugly as sin, a nine-shot cap and ball chambered in forty caliber with a sixty-two-caliber smoothbore barrel which also served as a cylinder latch pin, beneath the pistol barrel. The smoothbore carried either a musket ball or shotgun charge. Loaded with either it was a nasty close-quarter weapon. A sliding pin on the hammer shifted the firing mechanism from revolver cylinder to the smoothbore barrel. The LeMat was poorly balanced, awkward to the hand, heavy, and a man not used to the gun had almost no chance of making a hit. The weapon fit comfortably in Deacon's hand, though. He flipped the barrel selector a couple of times, then fished in a pocket and found two silver dollars.

"It's worth the price," he said, putting the coins on the counter. "You do good work, friend," he said. "Slick as goose grease. Feels brand-new."

The gunsmith nodded his thanks at the compliment. "Mind if I ask you something?"

"Go ahead."

"Why keep an old relic like this one? Barrel's near shot out. You could get a new Dragoon for what you'll spend on keeping that LeMat working over next year or two."

Deacon smiled at the gunsmith and patted the ugly pistol. "We been through a lot together. Reckon we'll keep each other company a while longer. Good gun's like a good horse or good woman. You find one that fits and you keep it 'til one or the other of you wears out."

The gunsmith chuckled. "And you wind up with a stove-up,

creaky old body, a wore-out gun, a swaybacked hoss and an ugly, wrinkled old woman who raises hell every time a man takes a drink. I know. Got one of each myself. Good luck to you, friend."

"Thanks," Deacon said as he turned for the door. "Man can always use a little luck."

He swung aboard his blue roan gelding and headed toward home. "I reckon," he said to the horse, "that ought to be enough town time to hold us both a couple of months."

Olive Ranch
October 1870

Print Olive tugged the cinch tight on a nervous sorrel, his second mount of the day, and swiped a bandana over the trail grit on the back of his neck. He and his hands had been in the saddle since before dawn. The crew was scattered over the ranch to start cattle drifting back toward headquarters.

The gather seemed to be going well. In another few days he would be ready to start putting his brand on several hundred new calves dropped during the spring. By the first greening of the grass next year, the new stock would be big enough and strong enough to join his growing herd of market cattle for the drive to railhead.

The price of beef had topped thirty dollars a head. By the time Print's drive hit Kansas in early summer the steers and dry cows could be worth forty dollars on the hoof.

Print allowed himself an inward sigh of satisfaction. By the time the first snow flew he would be a wealthy man.

"Rider coming hard," Jim Kelly said at Print's side. The black man stared toward the south, stock saddle forgotten in his hand. "Looks like Bob."

Print muttered a low curse. He had told Bob half a dozen times not to run a horse toward the ranch. A couple of stunts like that could ruin a good mount. Every time you turned their heads toward home they'd try to grab the bit and run. Print Olive hated a barn-soured horse.

"Looks like little brother needs another butt-chewing," Print groused.

Bob Olive yanked the lathered, blowing horse to a stop at the corral gate.

"Dammit, Bob," Print scolded, "I told you not to run—"

"Some sonofabitch took a shot at me, Print!" Bob swung from the saddle, his young face twisted in fury.

"What?"

"Down south of the Middle Yegua. Somebody took a pop at me with a rifle." Bob stepped to his horse's rump and traced a finger along a bloody furrow across the animal's left hip. "Missed me, but grazed my horse."

Print clambered over the fence and was at Bob's side in two strides. He glanced at the horse's wound.

"Who did it?"

Bob shook his head. "Didn't see him. Didn't even have a chance to shoot back. When that bullet stung this horse he went loco. Almost bucked me off. By the time I had him lined out, we were a mile past the Yegua." Bob kicked in disgust at a pile of horse droppings. "I'd had half a chance I'd a' hunted that bushwhacking bastard down and killed him." Bob's hand fell to the butt of the Navy revolver at his waist.

"Most likely you'd just got yourself killed, Bob," Jim Kelly said. He had dropped his saddle, vaulted the rail fence and now stood beside Print, studying the bloody gouge on the horse's hip. "That looks like a big-bore rifle track to me," Kelly said. He turned to the younger Olive. "You could have rode smack into the next slug."

"I'd have got the bastard," Bob snapped. He started to toe the stirrup. "Let's go. We can still track him down."

"Not on that horse, you won't. He wouldn't make two miles." Print turned toward the barn. "Cortinas!"

The elderly chore man shuffled into view from a stable.

"Bring my dapple gray for Bob. *Andele.* Then take care of this horse." Print shoved the corral gate open. "Jim, we got any other hands around?"

Kelly shook his head as he reached for his saddle. "All out on the gather, boss."

"Then the three of us will go. By God, nobody takes a shot at an Olive and gets away with it. We'll track that sonofabitch down and hang him to the nearest oak. Saddle up. And don't waste any time about it."

Four hours later and three miles south of the ambush site, Jim Kelly knelt on a swath of hardpan and shook his head. "Can't track him over this stuff," he said in disgust. "Whoever it was, he's long gone now."

"Dammit," Bob snapped, "I thought you were a tracker!"

Print rammed his Henry back into the saddle sheath and glared at his younger brother. "Back off, Bob. Jim's the best tracker you'll ever meet. I won't have you bad-mouth him." He reined his sorrel about. "Come on, boys. We'll find the bushwhacker sooner or later. In the meantime we've got cattle to gather."

Deacon Scruggs shifted in the saddle, putting most of his weight on the left stirrup to ease the ache of the deep bruise on his right buttock.

He had taken a considerable hoorawing from the Olive cowhands over that bruise. Seemed like a man getting thrown from a green bronc on a cold morning was the funniest thing since Chad Bailey shot off his own toe showing his fast draw. Even Deacon had grinned about it a little at the time, but it didn't take long for a bruised butt against a hard saddle to lose a lot of its hilarity.

He rode a few feet to Print's left as the two scouted Antelope Flat for any cattle missed in the branding. The Flat was a halfmile swath of tall grass, singed now by first frost. It was free of timber except for a strip of scrub oaks and taller hardwood trees lining a small creek that cut across the meadow.

Deacon couldn't see how they could have missed many cattle in the fall roundup. The crew had put the Olive brand on better than a thousand calves and a half a hundred grown animals after the gather. He could still smell the hair and hide burning under the branding irons along with the delicate, rich aroma of testicles from freshly castrated calves roasting on a tin sheet at the edge of the branding fire. Some people turned pale at just the mention of mountain oysters. Roasted or fried, they were a delicacy to the men who rode the range. It was one of the things that made branding time a cowman's favorite season of the year.

Print abruptly pulled his horse to a stop. "Company," he said with a nod toward a line of scrub oaks thirty yards away. Deacon forgot his bruised butt and squared himself in the saddle. He hadn't detected any movement, but Print seemed to have a sixth sense about such things.

"Any idea who?"

"Somebody who has no business on this range." Print's hand rested on the butt of the big Remington revolver at his side, his brows bunched in anger. "Better get a hold on that old LeMat, Deacon," Print said through gritted teeth.

Deacon pulled the ugly revolver and began checking the caps. He glanced up when Print spat a bitter curse. A cow and yearling calf emerged from the trees. Deacon recognized the peculiar half-moon marking on the longhorn cow's face. She was an Olive cow.

Print nudged his horse forward. A horseman broke through the edge of the thicket, his right hand pushing aside a low-hanging branch, his attention on the cattle. Deacon's breath caught in his throat. The rider was Deets Phreme.

Print's horse nickered. Phreme glanced up, seemed to flinch in the saddle, then fixed his gaze on the Olive riders as his hand dropped to the grips of the pistol at his waist. Instead of wheeling his horse and fleeing into the relative safety of the grove, Phreme reined his mount toward the approaching men. Deacon heard Print's steady stream of muttered curses as the distance between the horsemen closed to within twenty feet.

"Damn your soul, Phreme," Print said, "I told you never to show your face on Olive land again!"

"And I told you it ain't over between us, Olive." Phreme's tone was sharp and hard. Hate glittered in the narrowed eyes behind angry scars. Deacon kneed his mount to Print's left and thumbed the selector on the LeMat hammer to the shotgun barrel. The smoothbore was loaded with buckshot, deadly at close range.

For a few seconds Print Olive and Deets Phreme faced each other in silence, each with his hand on the butt of a pistol, the tension building.

"Are you the dirty bastard who shot at my brother?" A black fury tinged Print's voice.

"No, by God—but I'd sure as hell like to take a pop at you!"

The two men drew at the same instant. Print's horse shied from the sudden movement, into Deacon's line of fire. Two gunshots sounded almost as one. Deacon heard the air burst from Print's lungs and saw him twist in the saddle. Over Print's shoulder Deacon saw Phreme jerk backward and tumble over his horse's rump. Print slapped another shot toward the fallen man, fighting his skittish mount.

"Kill the sonofabitch, Deacon!" Print gasped. "He got lead into me." He slumped in the saddle. Deacon glimpsed a smear of red low on Print's back.

Deacon yanked his horse around Print, the LeMat pointed at Phreme as he approached the downed rider. Phreme lay face up in the grass. A single bullet hole pulsed blood from the center of Phreme's shirt pocket. Phreme's eyes were already beginning to glaze. His boots cribbed at the soil in a jerky death dance.

Deacon lowered the hammer of the LeMat, jammed it into the holster and kneed his mount alongside Print. The dark eyes that stared back at him were hazy with shock and the beginning of pain.

"He's dead, Print. You nailed him through the heart."

Print nodded and coughed. "Sonofabitch shot me, Deacon," he said in disbelief. "I didn't think—" His words ended in a gasp as the first real wave of agony ripped through his body. He lifted his hand from his side. The fingers were streaked with crimson. "Hit me—pretty hard."

Deacon helped Print dismount and ripped the bloody shirt aside. The heavy ball had hit Print just above the belt on the right side, passed through the soft flesh and came out halfway between backbone and hip. "How bad is it, Deacon?"

"Bad enough, Print. Could be the ball nicked a gut. Can't be sure." He slipped a hand under Print's shoulder and lowered the wounded man to a sitting position.

"Get me back—on my horse." Print's voice was weak, his face pale. His gaze drifted in and out of focus; the Remington slipped from his grip and fell at his feet.

"You're not ridin' a horse anywhere, Print Olive," Deacon

said. "You're bleedin' like a stuck pig. I'll patch you up best I can and fetch a wagon from the ranch."

Deacon stripped the kerchief from around his neck and pressed it against the hole in Print's back and used Print's bandana to cover the wound in front. He ripped Print's shirt in half and bound the kerchiefs in place. Print moaned. "It's—got awful cold, Deacon," he muttered. The dark eyes closed and Print's chin dropped to his chest.

"Hang on, friend," Deacon said, "we'll get you back home." He eased Print to a prone position, untied the slicker from the back of his saddle and draped it over Print. The black eyes fluttered open.

"Pistol," Print said, his voice barely audible.

Deacon picked up Print's fallen Remington and placed it in his hand. Then he mounted his horse and spurred for the ranch.

SEVEN

Olive Ranch
October 1870

Print Olive woke to searing pain, as if a red-hot branding iron had been rammed through his right side. He heard a low moan, realized it had been his own and tried to sit up. The movement triggered a fresh blast of agony and a wave of nausea. He gave up trying to move. It wasn't worth it. For a moment he lay with his eyes closed, confused, unsure of where he was or what had happened.

Something warm and wet pressed against his forehead. He opened his eyes and blinked against the flare of lamplight. Louise sat in a chair at his bedside, her face more pale and drawn than Print remembered it.

"Print? Are you awake?"

Print groaned through clenched teeth. A heavy weight seemed to mash against his right side. The pain lessened for a few seconds, then came back in a fresh explosion. Print's breath whistled through his teeth. He closed his eyes. The rising tide of pain triggered bits and pieces of memory—the encounter on the flat, the slam of a bullet into his body, the prickle of straw on a jolting wagon bed and the bone-shaking chills which came on the heels of almost unbearable heat that left the sheets beneath him soaked in sweat.

He felt Louise's palm against his stubbled cheek.

"The fever seems to be breaking," Louise said. "Doctor Havemayer says that means the worst should be past."

Print tried to speak. The words came out a hollow croak through parched lips.

"Hush, Print. Just rest now. I'll get the doctor. He's waiting in the parlor."

Moments later Dr. Willis Havemayer leaned over the bed, pried open one of Print's eyelids, stared and grunted. Havemayer probed his fingers under the wide bandage around Print's side. Print gasped at the touch.

"Hang in there, Print," Havemayer said in a baritone that seemed out of place in the narrow chest. "You're in pretty good shape, considering." Havemayer lifted Print's head and placed a cup at his lips. Print sucked eagerly at the liquid. "Easy, now," the doctor said. He lowered the cup. "That water's laced with tincture of opium. It'll ease the pain in a few minutes. Take too much at once and you'll finish what Deets Phreme started."

A sudden, cold terror grabbed Print's chest. He had seen gut-shot men in the war. It was a slow and agonizing way to die. "How—how bad—"

Havemayer removed the small half-spectacles from the bridge of his nose and wiped at them with a handkerchief. He cocked an eyebrow at Print.

"You came out pretty lucky. The slug went in through the lumbar muscles, nicked the large intestine—I had to cut on you a little to get that patched up—but it missed the major blood vessels. It passed within an inch of your right kidney and came out through the lower back muscles about three inches from your spine. The slug didn't expand much."

Havemayer replaced the spectacles and peered over the top of the lenses at Print. "The only thing we have to worry about now is infection. I haven't seen any signs of that yet. You're going to hurt like hell for a while, but you're young and strong. If all goes well you should be back on your feet in a few weeks."

The physician lifted the cup and allowed Print another small sip. "You've got a couple of good nurses in Louise and Anna Maria. I'll leave them instructions and some of this tincture. Ask for it when the pain gets bad enough you don't think you can stand it any longer, but don't abuse it. I've had patients get hooked on this stuff like a channel cat on a throwline. Went through absolute raging hell when they ran out of it."

Print felt his eyelids begin to sag. The pain had all but subsided. The combined effect of the opiate, the doctor's soothing baritone and his own weakness had pushed him near the edge of sleep.

"The cattle—"

"Don't worry about the ranch, Print Olive." The doctor's voice seemed to come from a distance. "Ira's got everything under control. Behave yourself and you won't miss that spring drive to railhead . . ." Havemayer's voice faded completely.

Georgetown
January 1871

Print Olive shifted his weight in the hard wooden chair at the defense table, trying to ease the stiffness in his right side. The wound was healing, but slowly, and now it nagged at him in protest over the long buggy ride to the county seat.

At his side, attorney W. K. Makemson slipped a confident wink in Print's direction. District Judge Houston Sullivan stroked his muttonchop whiskers in thought, his long fingers fiddling with a pen.

"Mister Makemson," the judge said, "you have advanced a reasonable argument for continuance in this case." The judge pointed the pen at Print as if it were a rifle. "I still have some reservations about you, Mister Olive. Your record to date shows five convictions—"

"Your honor," Makemson interrupted, "those incidents were all misdemeanors and should have no bearing—"

"Mister Makemson, you don't have to tell me the law. I have a reasonable grasp of legal concepts. Now, if I may continue?" The judge glared at the attorney. Makemson flushed and fell silent. "Mister Olive, you've been in court several times. One assault case was dismissed, I see. On four occasions you paid one dollar fines for assault. You've paid fines for disturbing the peace, brawling, and firing a gun within town limits."

The judge lowered the pen and tapped it against the bench. "However, you have no felony convictions. I will, therefore, rule favorably on your motion. Trial in the case of the State of Texas versus Isom Prentice Olive on a charge of murder in the death of

Deets Phreme, also known as D. R. Phreme and by other names, is hereby set for the next session of this court a year from now."

Judge Sullivan dropped the pencil and picked up his worn gavel. "In view of your plan for a cattle drive to Kansas, Mister Olive, I am going to allow you to remain free on continuance of your five-hundred-dollar bond. I admonish you, however, that I expect you to complete your business and return to this court on the first week in March 1872, to answer to these charges. I concur with Mister Makemson's arguments that a man with your extensive holdings and strong ties to the county will not jump bail and head for the badlands."

Print bit back the urge to comment. *Dammit,* he thought in disgust, *there's no reason a man should even have to stand trial for killing a sonofabitch like Phreme; the county ought to buy me a fresh supply of ammunition instead.* He nodded his acceptance of the conditions.

"Thank you, your honor," Makemson said. "I assure you my client will appear as scheduled."

"Yes, Mister Makemson, he will. Or I will have your hide along with his." Sullivan thumped the gavel against a hardwood block. "Call the next case."

Makemson led the way from the courtroom. Outside, a handful of curious onlookers cast nervous glances at the dozen heavily armed Olive riders waiting beside the buggy. Print shook Makemson's hand, declined the lawyer's offer of a cigar and climbed stiffly into the buggy. "See you in a year, W.K.," he said.

He tapped the reins against the bay mare's rump. The buggy jolted into motion. The movement sent a twinge of discomfort through Print's side.

"You sure you're up to driving that rig, Print?" Deacon Scruggs rode at the side of the buggy, rifle nested in the crook of an elbow. "I'd be glad to take the reins."

Print shook his head. "No, Deacon. Maybe I can't fork a horse yet, but I can drive a buggy."

Print drew in a deep breath, enjoying the sharp bite of winter honed by a north wind that pushed low gray clouds overhead. The chill was a welcome thing after weeks of lying in bed, bedeviled by women, then caged inside a house and creaking around on a cane like an old used-up bronc stomper. But he was healing. It wasn't long until spring. By then Print planned to be back in the saddle, leading a herd of cattle north. "Bet it's colder than hell in Kansas today, Deacon," Print said.

Little River, Kansas
May 1871

Print Olive reined Buckshot around to survey the herd which trailed behind him. He would have twisted his body in the saddle, but now such moves often brought a jabbing pain to his right side.

The cattle were about as trail tame as longhorns ever got, Print thought. The drive had gone well so far. Once the herd had settled down they had made ten to twelve miles a day. Print had left Williamson County with just over two thousand head, more than half of which were Olive cattle. The rest belonged to Dudley Snyder and Fred Smith.

Print and his drovers had lost a hundred head in a thunderstorm stampede south of the Red River. They left behind another hundred to bribe various tribes to let them cross Indian Territory along the old Chisholm Trail. But they had picked up over a hundred fifty strays along the way. Road-branded and added to the herd, the strays almost made up for the losses.

The cattle were strung out for more than two miles along the trail, grazing on the rich green prairie grass as they moved. The animals would be in fine shape at railhead in Ellsworth. Water had been adequate except for the past few days and Little River was just a couple of miles ahead. The river would be a welcome sight. Longhorns could travel for several days without water when they had to, but they started getting restless after the first couple of days.

Print rode the point, leading the herd. He had no trouble picking up the landmarks described by Dudley Snyder. If he had any doubts, he could always call on Smith's foreman, Cal Nutt, who had made the Ellsworth drive last year and rode now as the Smith ranch rep.

Behind Print the bell steers, trail wise and gentle, set the pace

for the rest of the herd. The bell steers wouldn't be sold at Ellsworth. They were too valuable a commodity. They had made the
trip twice with the Snyders and Fred Smith. They would be
trailed back home and treated well until called for service on the
next drive. One good bell steer was worth a half a dozen cowboys on the trail.

Jim Kelly rode the right flank. Rob Murday, who had turned
out to be a top hand around cows, had the left flank. Print was
pleased that he had decided not to kill Murday. It had been a
good decision for both of them. Riding swing were two Olive
hands, a Mexican and a Negro. Two of the Snyder cowboys, Bob
Olive and Deacon Scruggs joined other drovers hired just for
the drive in riding drag, pushing the more reluctant animals at
the rear of the herd.

Bob had bellyached about eating dust all the way from Texas,
but that was where hands new to the trail were assigned. Riding
drag was the lowest position in a trail crew's pecking order. It
was also the hardest and dirtiest job. Eventually Bob would move
up the unofficial ranks to swing, then flank, and finally point
when he became boss of his own outfit. Deacon never complained, and he had managed to keep Bob in line most of the
time. Counting the cook and horse wrangler, there were fifteen
men pointing the Olive herd north. Ira, Jay and most of the
regular Olive hands remained behind to care for the home livestock and start building a herd for the next drive.

Print grunted in satisfaction and reined Buckshot toward the
north.

A half mile later he pulled the horse to a stop. Three men
waited a hundred yards away, rifles resting across saddle horns.

Print studied the riders for a moment. He had been expecting
them. Not these three in particular, but some like them. It was
common practice in southern Kansas for settlers to lay claim to
water sources along the trails and charge fees to drovers for
watering their herds. Print knew some of the demands were
outrageous. He rolled a smoke, fired the quirly with a match
scraped across the saddle horn and casually kneed Buckshot forward.

"Howdy," the biggest of the three men said as Print stopped

his mount a few paces away. "Name's Cap Courson. These here men are my brothers. You the boss of that cow outfit yonder?"

Print nodded.

"New out here, ain't you?" Courson's grin bared stained and broken teeth. The man's bulging belly threatened to lap over the horn of his saddle. It was obvious to Print that Cap Courson hadn't hit a lick of work in quite some time.

Print stubbed his cigarette against his leggings and let the last shreds of tobacco fall. "First trip," he said, his voice calm. "Something I can do for you men?"

Cap Courson chuckled aloud. "Reckon it's what we can do for you, Texas. Them critters of yours need water. We got it. We own Little River for some good ways here."

Print touched the brim of his hat, keeping up the facade of an innocent in a strange land. "That's neighborly of you, Mister Courson."

"Just one catch here, Texas. You gotta pay for our water."

"Pay?"

"Yep. Ain't no other water for miles. Reckon you got no choice."

"How much for watering the herd?"

Courson shrugged. "Oh, I reckon a hundred dollars might cover it."

Print lifted his hat and scratched his head. He checked the anger that surged behind his belt buckle. "A hundred dollars seems a bit high to me, Mister Courson." The settler's face tightened in a scowl. "But," Print said, keeping his tone polite with a conscious effort, "I don't know that much about the customs here in Kansas. I'll have to get my financial manager up here to talk with you." He reined Buckshot about and waved his hat toward Jim Kelly.

Moments later the big black man pulled his bay to a stop at Print's side and glared at the Courson brothers. Cap Courson's eyes widened. Print had heard that few Kansans had ever seen a Negro before. Especially one with a big Dragoon Colt riding on his hip.

"Mister Courson, meet Jim Kelly. He's the man handles my financial negotiations." He turned to Jim and said casually,

"These gentlemen are asking a hundred dollars to water the herd."

A low growl started in the back of Jim Kelly's throat. His hand dropped to the Dragoon. Print heard Jim's molars begin to grind. Print turned his attention to Courson. The man's face had gone ash-white. Print waited, listening and watching, until he sensed the growing fear in the three horsemen. Jim was all but playing a tune with those grinding teeth. Print knew that by now Jim would have rolled his eyes until only the whites showed.

"Now, gentlemen, make your deal with Mister Kelly here." Print turned his head and spat. "Mister Kelly doesn't like it when someone tries to take advantage of us. He nearly killed one man back on the Red for trying to gouge us on the price of flour. Took four men to get him off. That was over just a couple dollars. And shoot? I've seen him drop a running antelope with a handgun at fifty, sixty yards. One shot. Right smack through the eye."

The gnashing of teeth was loud in the sudden silence that followed.

"Mister Courson," Print prodded, "I think you might want to negotiate. I'm not sure I can keep this big nigger under control."

The grinding stopped. Kelly's baritone rumbled, "You damn punkin' roller farmers ain't holdin' up this man for no hundred dollars." The ominous click of a Dragoon hammer drawn to full cock punctuated Kelly's words. "You want to try holdin' us up, use them rifles and do it proper. I'm tired of sweet-talkin' you bastards, and I'm gettin' mad."

"Easy, Jim. No need to kill all three of them." He raised an eyebrow at Courson. "Maybe you want to study on dropping that price some, Courson. I never know when this nigger's going to explode. He's got a hell of a temper."

Courson swallowed hard. "Twenty might do it." He stared wide-eyed at Jim Kelly. The low rumble sounded again. "Ten. Ten's enough. We got wives and kids . . ."

Print heard the raw fear in the man's tone. He held back the urge to smile.

"You gonna have some widows and orphans, damn your thieving souls," Kelly growled.

"Five! For God's sake, five!"

Print sighed in resignation. "Let it stand, Jim. I guess a man's got to feed his family. Five dollars seems fair—if that includes our horses, too."

Courson nodded. Print dug in his pocket, found a five-dollar gold piece and held it aloft. "And the water barrels on our chuck wagon." He kneed Buckshot alongside Courson and tucked the coin in the settler's shirt pocket. "One more thing, Mister Courson," he said, his voice soft, "I don't think we want any trouble from you or your brothers here while we're passing through. Jim Kelly here, he's the easygoing one in my crew."

Courson finally tore his eyes from the black man's face. "You won't have no trouble here, Texas."

Print slapped Courson lightly on the shoulder. "Now, I'm sure glad to hear that, sir. It's a pleasure to find such neighborly folks on our travels." He kneed Buckshot about. "Jim, let's go water some cattle."

The two men turned their backs on the three Kansans. When they had ridden out of earshot, Print chuckled. "Jim, you're some kind of work. It will be a long time before those three forget this day. There'll be a bonus for you when we hit Ellsworth."

Ellsworth, Kansas

Print Olive sat at the hexagonal mahogany table in a room off the bar of Beede's Hotel on Texas Street, a quart of Old Crow at his elbow and a small glass at his left hand. He studied the man seated across from him as the gambler raked in another pot.

The man's name was Jim Kennedy. Print wasn't sure if Kennedy was a top-notch poker player, a lucky bastard or a first-rate cheat. Print suspected the latter. But he couldn't figure how Kennedy was cheating and it wasn't polite to shoot a man on pure suspicion.

Four other men sat at the table—a merchant, a banker, the cattle buyer who had purchased Print's herd and Cal Nutt. Print didn't think Cal had any business in a high-stakes game, but it wasn't his place to tell a grown man what to do.

The deal went to the cattle buyer seated at Print's left. The "gentleman's game" had cost Print a hundred. His mood darkened with each losing hand.

The game in the Beede was a closed table, as opposed to the wide-open gambling for all comers at the saloons in the Scragtown section of Ellsworth. Scragtown was for cowboys, the Beede for cattlemen. The difference was mainly the amount of money involved and the lack of whores who caged drinks from drovers at trail's end.

The game was five-card draw. Print watched Kennedy cut, saw nothing out of the ordinary and waited as the cattle buyer dealt the cards.

The drive had ended as well as it began, Print thought. Even though his herd wasn't the first to reach railhead that season it was in the best flesh. The buyer's offer was a dollar a head better than Print expected. Print had a bank draft for better than twenty thousand dollars in his pocket.

Print picked up his hand, saw little hope in the cards and folded when the merchant opened. Print splashed a dollop of Old Crow into his glass and sipped at the drink. It was good whiskey, not like the swill the Texas cowboys called "Kansas Sheepdip" served in Scragtown, where most of his own crew had gathered to celebrate the end of the trail.

Print had no particular urge to join them. He had his whiskey, and after so many weeks of being cooped up in that house while his side mended, he wasn't too keen on women right now. Cattle were a darn sight easier to manage, he thought. At least a man knew what they wanted.

He watched as Kennedy bet ten dollars after drawing two cards. The slender gambler in the silk shirt and blue suit was good at his trade. Cal Nutt folded his hand with a snort of disgust, pulled a watch from his pocket, flipped the lid and glanced at the time. The watch was Cal's only nonessential possession. It was the kind carried by railroad conductors. The lid sported an engraved buck deer head. Cal snapped the watch shut and dropped it back in his pocket. "It's getting late, and this game's too rich for my blood, boys," he said. Cal was a short, wiry man, stronger than he looked, with solidly muscled sloping shoulders, a square face with a solid jaw that looked stubbled even after a fresh shave. If there was any fear in the man Print had never seen it.

Print pushed the bottle of Old Crow to Cal. "Help yourself to a nightcap, Cal," he said, watching as Kennedy raked in another pot with a full house, sixes over fours. Cal lifted the bottle, poured a couple of ounces in his glass, then lifted the drink. "To a good drive, Print—and a good future for us both."

Print tilted his glass to return the toast and tossed back the contents. The liquor warmed his stomach and chased the stiffness from his side. He picked up the deck and began to shuffle the cards.

Cal pushed back from the table and reached for his hat as the door of the gaming room swung open. Deacon Scruggs was at Print's side in two long strides. "Trouble, Print."

"What now?"

"It's Bob. He got in a fight with one of the hands from the YO outfit over some whore. Bob shot him."

"Kill him?"

"No. Just winged him. Not much more than a scratch."

Print sighed in disgust. "Dammit, I told that kid to leave his gun in the room. You'd think by now he'd at least learned to shoot. Where is he?"

"Town marshal's got him. Fixin' to charge him with attempted murder and lock him up."

Print tossed the cards on the table and shoved his chair back. "Where's the man he shot?"

"Doc's office. Two doors down from the lockup."

"I'll take care of it, Deacon," Print said. "You gather up the rest of the boys. Tell the ones who want to go back to Texas with us that we're leaving at first light." He stared for a moment at the gambler across the table. "Kennedy, if you're still around next time I come through, I'll see you again. And I'll figure out then exactly what your game is."

Kennedy flushed. "What do you mean by that, Olive?"

"Make it what you want, Kennedy."

Print spun on a heel and stalked from the hotel, Cal Nutt at his side.

Bob Olive sat with his head in his hands in the town marshal's office as Print walked in, accompanied by a young cowboy whose arm was in a sling.

"Bob, I warned you about this sort of thing," Print said, his tone sharp.

Bob looked up. One eye was swollen almost shut. He held a handkerchief to a cut seeping blood over the eye. He started out of his chair, fist balled, cursing the cowboy. Print put a hand on his shoulder and rammed him back into the seat. "Sit down and keep your mouth shut, Bob. I'll handle this."

The marshal, a weathered man with a heavy gray mustache, glanced up from his desk. "Who are you, mister?"

"Print Olive. That's my brother you're holding. I came to take him home."

"Won't be easy, Mister Olive. There's a charge against him."

Print nodded toward the cowboy at his side. "This is the man he shot. He's agreed not to press charges."

The marshal leaned back in his chair. "That right, Erickson?"

The cowboy nodded. "Yes, sir. I don't reckon it was his fault no more than mine."

The marshal snorted. "Son, if you don't care, I sure as hell don't. There's still the matter of a ten-dollar fine for disturbing the peace, Mister Olive."

Print plucked a gold piece from his pocket and dropped it on the marshal's desk. "That all, Marshal?"

"I suppose so." The lawman reached into a desk drawer, pulled out Bob's Navy revolver and belt and handed the rig to Print. "See if you can keep that thing away from him until you're out of my town, Mister Olive," he said. He turned to the bandaged cowboy. "Are you absolutely sure you don't want to press charges?"

The young man swallowed nervously and winced in pain. "Yes, sir. I'm sure."

"All right. You're all free to go. But you two young whelps remember that the next time you're in Ellsworth, I don't want to see either of you even spit on the sidewalk. Do we have an understanding?"

Bob glared at the cowhand through his one good eye and managed a surly nod.

Five minutes later, Print and Bob strode back toward the hotel. "Dammit, Bob!" Print snapped. "I've got all the worries I can handle without you getting in a storm every half hour. I had to give that cowboy fifty dollars not to leave you stuck in some Kansas jail. I tell you, little brother, I'm a tad put out with you."

"Gimme my gun," Bob muttered through swollen lips.

"Like hell I will. You'll get it back when you need it." Print stared at Bob's battered face. "You better learn something out of this, Bob. You can't fistfight for sour apples—and you don't shoot so damn fine either. Now, let's get to bed. We're heading home at first light."

EIGHT

Georgetown, Texas
March 1872

Deacon Scruggs squirmed on the hard witness chair in the district courtroom and hoped his jangling nerves didn't show. He was as scared as he had been at any time during the war. Wars fought with guns he understood. Wars fought with words got confusing.

"And that, Mister Scruggs," attorney W. K. Makemson said, "is when the gunfight between the defendant, Isom Prentice Olive, and the deceased, Deets Phreme, occurred?"

"Yes, sir." Deacon glanced around the crowded courtroom. The place was jammed, mostly with Print Olive's relatives, friends and hired hands. The few observers who fancied themselves enemies of the Olives looked nervous and uncomfortable in the crowd.

Old Man James Crow and his eldest son, recently released from prison, stood with Turk Turner just inside the door. The three twitched at strange noises and flinched when an Olive rider moved. They looked, Deacon thought, as though they would tear down half the door getting out if Print turned around and said boo.

"Who was the first to draw a weapon?"

"They drew near at the same time," Deacon said, aware of a trickle of sweat down his back. "There was two gunshots, sort of one on top of the other, real quick."

"And both Print Olive and Deets Phreme were hit?"

"Yes, sir. Print—Mister Olive—got shot in the side. Phreme got hit in the heart. He died real quick."

Makemson turned aside. "Would you say, Mister Scruggs, that it was a fair fight?"

"Near as there is such a thing, yes, sir."

"And that Print Olive was justified in shooting Deets Phreme?"

"Yes, sir. He—Phreme—was stealin' our cows. He got caught. He cussed at Print and pulled his pistol. Man's got a right to defend his life and property."

"Thank you, Mister Scruggs." Makemson turned to the judge. "Your honor, in view of this man's eyewitness account and the testimony presented here earlier by Mister Henry Pelsworth and others implicating Deets Phreme in organized cattle thefts, I request the court instruct the jury to return a verdict of not guilty."

Judge Houston Sullivan nodded toward the prosecutor, a slender, pale young man fresh out of law school. The judge and everyone else in the county knew the young lawyer owed his appointment to the influence of the Olives and their friends, the Snyders and Fred Smith. His pursuit of the case against Print had been less than vigorous. "Does the prosecution wish to examine the witness or to present further evidence?"

"No, your honor."

"You may step down, Mister Scruggs." The judge waited until Deacon moved away and wedged himself into a spot along a wall. Sullivan cleared his throat. "In view of the fact that the prosecution has failed to provide sufficient evidence to support the charge, this court hereby instructs the jury to return a not guilty verdict in the charge against Isom Prentice Olive in the shooting death of Deets Phreme."

Judge Sullivan banged his gavel in an attempt to quiet the outburst of applause and yells of triumph that swept the courtroom. A couple of the whoops came from the jury box, where two of Dudley Snyder's hands sat. *Old Print sure knows how to stack a legal deck,* Deacon thought. *Even if it had gone to the jury, there wasn't a chance in hell Print would be convicted.* Deacon was learning a lot about the power of money here lately.

The judge gave up his gavel banging and muttered a futile curse. "The jury is dismissed," he called above the din. "Court stands in recess until after lunch."

The crowd surged toward Print, eager to offer congratulations. Deacon shifted his gaze toward the door. Turner and the Crows had disappeared. *Got to remind Print to watch our backs on the way home,* Deacon told himself. Deacon waited until the crowd had thinned and Print started toward the door, then fell into step alongside his employer and friend.

"What now, Print?" he asked.

Print smiled. "We go back to the cow business. Ira's already pointed a herd north. Jay's got another bunch about ready to go. We can have them in Kansas by fall."

Deacon sighed in relief at the news. He had never been one for town life in the first place. And now would be a good time to get Print back on the trail and away from Williamson County. It didn't take but one man with a rifle and a mad on to pop a slug in a man's back.

"Besides," Print said, his tone grim, "I've got a rematch at the poker table with that Jim Kennedy in mind. That card sharp cheated me. This time I'm going to catch him at it."

Ellsworth, Kansas
September 1872

Print Olive sat in the same chair of the gaming room in Beede's Hotel, the whiskey glass at his elbow untouched except for a sip every half hour. Print knew he would need all his faculties sharp to catch Kennedy cheating.

Jim Kelly lounged against the bar set up for the convenience of the players a couple of strides from the table, watching the play. He held a glass in his left hand and his right seldom strayed from the Dragoon at his hip. Jim was Print's down-card ace in a game that could turn deadly.

The game tonight was five card stud. It had cost Print eighty dollars before he picked up Kennedy's overall strategy. The gambler let the other players pick up the lesser pots most of the time. Then on Kennedy's third or fourth deal, good hands would turn up around the table, most of them built around face cards. On the final card, with the betting heavy, Kennedy would deal himself a low-spot card—and usually fill four of a kind or a small full house, just good enough to win.

Print had dropped another hundred since then, but now he had set his trap. On his last deal, Print had palmed the seven of clubs and slipped it under his belt. All he had to do now was wait and hope the gambler couldn't tell from the feel of the deck that a card was missing. Print doubted that he would. Kennedy was not only good at his trade, he was smug enough to figure no one would tumble to his tricks.

Kennedy, seated across from Print, had the deal. And he was due. Print felt his heartbeat quicken as Kennedy dealt the first two rounds of cards, one down, one up. Print had a queen in the hole and another lady up; the cattle buyer at his right had an ace up and the banker at his left had a king showing. Kennedy's up card was the seven of hearts.

The cattle buyer opened for ten dollars. Print promptly raised another ten. The betting became more heated with each card until better than four hundred was on the table with a card to go. Print filled his full house, queens over jacks, on the last card. The banker had a pair of kings showing, the cattle buyer two aces up. Kennedy showed three sevens and the four of hearts.

Print casually tossed a hundred dollars on the table. The banker and cattle buyer stayed. Kennedy called and raised. *The bastard's done it,* Print thought; *he's finally made his mistake.* The pot was over a thousand dollars when the betting ended.

Kennedy turned up his hole card. It was the seven of clubs. The gambler chuckled and reached for the pot. "Seems to be my night, gentlemen," he said. "Lady luck came through for me with that fourth seven."

"I'd say luck had nothing to do with it, Kennedy," Print said.

The gambler's eyes narrowed. "What are you saying, Mister Olive?"

"I'm saying that you're slick. I still don't know how you did it, but explain this to us." He flicked the club seven from beneath his belt onto the table. "There weren't four sevens in that deck." Print kicked back his chair and started to rise, his hand reaching for the Remington.

The gambler's hand dropped beneath the table. Three sharp reports sounded. Print felt a fist slam into his leg, another into his crotch. He staggered at the impact, still clawing at the Remington. Four other shots thundered in the small room. Kennedy's body jerked and the gambler toppled from his chair to the floor. Print glanced at Jim Kelly and saw the Dragoon in Kelly's fist through the haze of powder smoke. Print's hand fell away from the Remington. Pain lanced up his leg. "Bastard won't cheat anybody else," Print muttered. He felt Kelly's hand beneath his armpit.

"He got a couple into you, boss," Kelly said. "Somebody fetch a doctor."

Print Olive awoke to a fire that started at his belt and raged up and down his body. A few moments passed before he could focus his vision and orient himself. Jim Kelly's ebony face gradually blended into shape. Beyond Kelly, the mustached city marshal was speaking with the cattle buyer. Print felt a stab of fresh pain and heard the distinct click as a lead slug dropped into a metal container. He became aware of another presence, a stocky man with a flushed face and bloody hands.

"What—"

"Take it easy, Print," Kelly said. "It's not as bad as we thought. Kennedy had a belly gun. One of them little cloverleaf thirty-two rimfires."

The stocky man dropped his bullet probe into a tray. "You're a lucky man, Mister Olive," he said. "One slug hit you high in the thigh, but just tore up a little muscle. Another hit you in the groin. Two inches lower and to your left and you'd have been squatting to pee from now on. Would have ended your love life for sure, too." The doctor dribbled clear liquid over a swab. "This may sting a bit."

Print gasped as the raw alcohol hit torn flesh.

"You might have a cracked pelvic bone, but I doubt it," the doctor said as he swabbed the wounds. "Thirty-two rimfire doesn't pack that much punch. Kennedy was probably trying to get one in your gut, which would have been a skunk of a whole 'nuther stripe. You should recover."

"Kennedy?"

The doctor shook his head. "Your man here walloped him

with four big lead balls from a Dragoon at close range. That's a tad more firepower than you caught."

The marshal appeared at Print's side. "Mister Olive," the lawman said, disgust tinging his tone, "I can't charge you with anything. Kennedy pulled first. I'll fine your man here a dollar for firing a gun in the city limits and that'll be the end of it. But I would appreciate it if you decided to take your cows and your gambling to somebody else's town next time. You and your boys are starting to test my patience."

Print nodded, took a couple of hefty swigs from the bottle of Old Crow that Kelly lifted to his lips and waited for the warmth of the liquor to cut the pain. "We won't trouble you again, Marshal," he said. "Railhead's moving west anyway, and I got what I came for. No man cheats Print Olive twice."

Lawrence Chapel
January 1873

Jim Olive eased the buggy mare to a stop in front of his general store, his normally placid face drawn into a frown. Buckshot, Print's favorite horse, stood at the hitchrail along with Dudley Snyder's big Tennessee bay and Fred Smith's wiry little Spanish-type mustang.

Jim knew he had good and sufficient reason to frown. Print was collecting lead faster than a smelter. Even though he seemed recovered from the wounds at Ellsworth, he still winced from time to time at a pain in his side. Jim wasn't sure how long Print's luck was going to hold if he kept stopping bullets.

And Print wasn't the least of his family worries.

Young Bob was a genuine heller, worse than Print ever had been. Keeping Bob out of jail had gotten to be almost a full-time job and an expensive one. Twice in the last two months, Jim had paid fines for Bob—once for pistol-whipping a German farmer who objected to Print's laying claim to land which included the farmer's road and once for firing a pistol in downtown Round Rock. Jim also had bought a horse he didn't want or need, a two-year-old colt. Bob had taken a shine to the colt. He took the colt, too. If the owner hadn't been a friend and agreed to sell the animal at a fair price, Bob Olive would be in the Georgetown lockup now. *That boy's headed for no good,* Jim thought. *Between him and Print, we're headed for grief soon enough.*

Jim had given up his faint hope that Print would settle down to raising a family. God knows he had enough money. Three trail drives a year had snaked from the Olive range to railhead during the past three seasons. Each drive netted more profit than the last. And the number of cattle on Print's land hadn't shown that much of a decline despite the traffic between his ranch and Kansas. That fact hadn't escaped a lot of ranchers and farmers in the county.

Print ignored the rumors that some of his stock wore questionable brands. Jim also tried to ignore the rumors, unwilling to accept the idea that one of his sons might be a common cow thief. But it had gradually dawned on Jim that the arithmetic wasn't right, and Jim had always put a lot of faith in numbers. On rare occasions a longhorn cow might have twins. A whole herd sure didn't.

Jim climbed from the buggy and anvil-hitched the mare alongside the saddle horses. The cattle business, he thought, was not the end of his worries. He had lost several good customers over the past few months, mostly settlers. Solid, honest, God-fearing, churchgoing men and women. They had given lame excuses for no longer trading at the Olive store, but Jim knew that the truth was in a growing fear. A fear of his two sons, Print and Bob, and the violence that seemed to shadow them. Jim didn't miss the money all that much. Most of the settlers had little to spend. He did miss the people. They were nice folks.

Jim strode through the cluttered store to the back room where excess supplies were stored. The room was heavy with cigarette and cigar smoke and overly warm from the fire in the small stove.

Print sat on a keg, Dudley and Fred on boxes. The three nodded a greeting to Jim.

"It's getting worse, Print," Dudley said, his tone bitter. "One of my prize Tennessee studs was cut the other day—castrated like a yearling and left standing in my horse pasture. I've lost nearly a hundred head of cattle. Twenty of them were just killed and skinned out."

Fred grunted an agreement, rolling his cigar between thin but strong fingers. "Same with me. Somebody cut open one of my mares, yanked the unborn foal out and left the mare to die. There's forty head of my cows unaccounted for. Hiders killed and skinned another six. Somebody took a shot at one of my hands yesterday, not a mile from my house. I don't mind telling you I'm more than a little worried."

"By God, we can put a stop to it with a few good funerals." Print's face was flushed in anger.

"Who do we stop, Print? We don't even know who's behind it." Fred's tone was fatalistic. "It could be one of the granger bunch. Or some other gang. Until we know for sure, we're out on a limb."

"It's more than livestock now," Dudley said to Print. "Old Man Pelsworth testified against Deets Phreme at your trial. Two days ago, his mules pulled his wagon up to his house. Pelsworth was under the seat, cut nearly in half by a double load of buck-shot."

Print's eyes narrowed. "Phreme got his backing from Turner and Crow. I reckon that's the answer."

Jim Olive cleared his throat. "It's not that simple, Print. We have no idea who pulled those triggers."

"Our thinking," Fred Smith said cautiously, "is that maybe we better pull in our horns a little bit. You especially, Print. This trouble all started on your range."

Print glared at Fred for several heartbeats. "What are you saying, Fred? That it's my fault?"

"I'm saying nothing like that." Fred swallowed nervously. "I'm just saying that maybe if we don't expand our herds and lands more, if we just lie low, maybe it will blow over—"

"Dammit, Fred, I thought I counted you among my friends. I don't like what you're saying."

"I'm still a friend, Print. I just don't want to see any more grief."

"And you, Dudley?"

Dudley Snyder shrugged. "I don't know, Print. Maybe Fred's right, maybe not."

Print snorted in disgust. "All right, dammit. You two cut and run with your tails between your legs. I sure as hell won't. No bunch of dirt farmers is going to stop Print Olive. As far as I'm concerned this meeting is over." He stood and stalked out.

Fred Smith shrugged as the front door slammed. "It was worth a shot. I just wish Print wasn't so hardheaded." He turned to Jim Olive. "Jim, I want you to know that Dudley and I don't hold you to account for anything that's happened. You're a good man, and except for Print and Bob, you have a fine family. We don't want to see you and Julia hurt when all hell breaks loose around here. If you could talk some sense into Print . . ."

Jim Olive sighed. "Gentlemen, I lost control of that boy many years ago."

Jim waited until the two riders had left. Then he extinguished the fire in the stove, locked the front door and stood for a moment in the unseasonably warm winter sun. It didn't ease the chill in his heart.

Round Rock Road
February 1873

Print Olive pounded the hand-lettered sign into place with a fist-sized rock. It was the last of a half-dozen signs that now stood on the main trails leading into or through Print's landholdings.

The signs, printed in bold block letters, read:

ALL CATTLE AND HORSE THIEVES
PAY ATTENTION. ANYONE CAUGHT RIDING
AN OLIVE HORSE OR DRIVING
AN OLIVE COW
WILL BE SHOT ON SIGHT.

Print stepped back to check his handiwork. The sign listed a bit to the left but the message was straight enough. "That ought to let everybody know how the skunk ate the chicken," he muttered aloud.

Print stepped into the saddle and reined Buckshot back toward home. A slow anger still smoldered in Print over the meeting in his father's store. Dudley Snyder and Fred Smith had a lot of nerve, he grumbled inwardly, trying to tell a man how to run his business. He did feel better about Dudley since their last encounter a week ago on the open range. Dudley assured Print he was still an Olive ally. He still ran stock on Olive range. He would stand by the Olives if any big troubles came. Print wasn't so sure about Fred Smith. He had seen a sign of weakness in Fred during that meeting, and Williamson County was no place for a man with a yellow stripe in these times—

Print heard the solid whop of lead against flesh; a split second later the whipcrack of a rifle muzzle blast shattered the silence. Buckshot staggered and his front legs folded. Print kicked free of the stirrups as the horse went down. He landed hard on his left side as the animal fell. For a moment he lay stunned, the breath knocked from his lungs by the impact with the ground. Then he gasped air back into his chest and lunged over the dying horse, using the downed animal for cover. Blood spurted from a bullet-severed artery in the horse's neck. Print struggled to free his rifle trapped beneath Buckshot's body. The weapon finally pulled free.

Print cocked the Henry and stared toward a timbered hillside two hundred yards away. He thought he glimpsed a wisp of gunsmoke amid the trees and slapped a shot toward the spot. The shot brought no response. As the echo of the gunfire rolled away Print heard the clatter of hooves in the distance.

"Come back here, damn your bushwhacking soul!" Print yelled. "You want to fight, let's get on with it!"

The only sound along the trail was the death flail of hooves against sand as Buckshot died.

Print lay behind the horse's body for a half hour, senses strained to the breaking point. He scarcely dared breathe as he watched and listened. He decided there had been only one rifleman on the hill. If there had been more than one he would be in a fight for his life by now.

Print stood, crouched low, still alert, letting the black rage boil in his gut. The light northerly breeze carried no warning. A bobwhite quail chirped its two-note call from the copse of trees where the gunman had set up his ambush. Another quail answered. The birds would not have called if a man were nearby.

Print lowered the hammer of the Henry and stood, trembling in silent rage. Then he loosened the cinches, pulled his saddle free of the dead horse and stripped off the bridle. He wasn't about to leave his equipment for some dirt farmer or drifter to steal before he could get back to retrieve it.

He stood for a moment and stared at the body of the brown horse. "Dammit, Buckshot," he half whispered, "why is it always the good horses that get hurt and never the sorry ones?"

Print hefted the saddle and bridle onto his left shoulder, the Henry in his right hand. Pain stabbed through his right side where Phreme's slug had hit. His leg, still tender from the gambler's bullet, started to ache before he had made a dozen steps.

It was going to be a long walk back home.

NINE

Mustang Creek
April 1875

Deacon Scruggs knelt at the edge of the rain-swollen stream and studied the tracks in the damp sand.

"I make it three horses," Deacon said. "Maybe a dozen cattle. Not more than an hour old."

Print Olive nodded, his features grim. "You're getting good at reading sign, Deacon." Print drew his Remington and checked the loads and caps, sheathed the handgun and slid his Henry from its scabbard. "Let's go. It's judgment time for three rustlers. Even if they didn't know the rules before, they rode past one of our signs on the way in."

Deacon mounted and followed as Print nudged his horse into a ground-covering trot.

The raiders had come in from the southwest, gathered the stock, and now rode northeast toward San Gabriel. Print had often said he suspected San Gabriel to be the place where rustled stock—his own and that of other big ranchers in the county— changed hands and then disappeared. Deacon couldn't argue that reasoning. He had tracked stolen Olive stock almost to San Gabriel itself before losing the trail. The price of cattle kept going up, and with every dollar increase another dozen cow thieves seemed to turn up in Williamson County.

As he rode, Deacon checked the loads in the LeMat. High humidity sometimes fouled the powder or caps. Deacon didn't want any misfires today. He dropped the LeMat back into its holster.

They rode for the better part of an hour before Print checked his horse and pointed toward a meadow ahead. Three men trailed a small group of cattle across the open stretch of fresh spring grass. Deacon recognized several of the cows. He would have known them without the Olive brand on their hips.

"I know that bastard on the sorrel." Print's eyes held the look of a Comanche sizing up a white captive. "That's McDonald. He's tight with Turner and Crow's bunch. Could be he's the one took a shot at me and killed my best horse. He carries a big-bore Springfield." Print's gaze left the riders, flicked over the landscape ahead. The trail the men followed skirted a stand of timber. "We'll flank them. Hit them when they come out on the other side of the trees. McDonald's mine." Print cocked the Henry. "You take your pick of the other two. Let's go feed some buzzards."

Fifteen minutes later Deacon sat astride his big roan at one side of the faint trail, the LeMat cocked and ready. The lower barrel carried a soft lead sixty-one-caliber musket ball. At close range it would drop a horse in its tracks or knock a man halfway into the next county. He thumbed the barrel selector to smoothbore. Twenty yards away, Print Olive knelt at the base of a pecan tree, the Henry already at his shoulder.

Deacon's pulse quickened as the first of the longhorns moved into the open. The cow swung her head, snorted at the unexpected sight of a horseman, and bolted. The rest of the spooked cattle followed. The small herd thundered away from Deacon, tails thrown over the backs like a figure nine. Deacon heard a startled curse from the rear of the herd and the thud of horses' hooves. He lifted the LeMat.

The first rider cleared the timber. He yanked his mount to a sudden stop in shock and surprise at the sight of a big man horseback at the side of the trail. The rider grabbed for the pistol stuck in his waistband.

Deacon squeezed the trigger. The LeMat slammed back into his palm. The heavy slug caught the rider in the chest; the man seemed suspended in midair as his horse bolted from under him. The man fell heavily to the ground.

Deacon winced as a second rider kneed his mount toward him. Deacon saw the muzzle flash from a weapon and a slug hummed past his ear. He thumbed the barrel selector to revolver, steadied his aim and squeezed the trigger. The second man swayed, stayed in the saddle for twenty yards, then fell.

Deacon heard the crack of Print's Henry and turned his head in time to see McDonald sag over his horse's neck. McDonald recovered his balance and spurred the sorrel toward a brushy ravine. Print's rifle barked again and Deacon heard the whack of the slug against saddle leather. He thumbed the LeMat as rapidly as he could and sent three slugs toward the fleeing horseman, knowing as he pulled the trigger that the shots had gone wide.

Deacon chanced a glance toward Print. "Get the sonofabitch!" Print yelled as he levered a fresh load into the Henry and started to mount. Deacon whirled his horse in pursuit of the fleeing rider.

The chase lasted three miles through brush and muddy creeks. At first Deacon and Print seemed to be gaining ground. Then McDonald reached the open, level flats beyond the watershed. McDonald's horse was a blooded Kentucky racer, much faster than the cow horses the Olive men rode.

Print finally called a halt to the pursuit and reined in his stumbling and lathered mount. "I hit him, Deacon," Print said bitterly, "and it was just like I'd tapped him with a cane or something." Print glowered in disgust at the rifle in his hand, then jammed the weapon back into the scabbard. "Dammit, I'm going to get me a rifle that'll stop somebody once and for all the first time." He pulled the Remington forty-four from his holster. "Let's go check on those jaspers you downed."

It didn't take a close check. The one hit by the musket ball had died before he hit the ground, his spine blown away. The other lay on his back, chest heaving as he battled to draw air into shattered lungs. A ball had torn into his body beneath the armpit. Pink spittle dribbled from the corner of the wounded man's mouth.

"God's sake—help me—"

Print ignored the plea and stared at the downed man. "Let's go, Deacon. This one won't last long, but he'll die hard. That's what a cow thief deserves. We've got some cattle to gather."

Print reined his horse in the direction the panicked longhorns had run. Deacon paused long enough to reload the fired chambers of the LeMat, then followed. He swallowed against the taste of bile at the back of his throat. The killing seemed harder now than it had during the war.

Olive Ranch

Williamson County Sheriff Delbert Holland paused a half mile from Print Olive's home and reached for the pint bottle in his saddle bags. His hand trembled as he pulled the cork and lifted the bottle to cracked, dry lips. His throat seemed constricted. He had to swallow twice to keep the raw whiskey down.

Del Holland didn't try to fool himself. He was scared. Bone-deep scared. It wasn't every day a man had to try to bite the hand that fed him. If Print Olive didn't kill him on sight, he sure wasn't going to look kindly on being arrested. Holland took another pull from the bottle and kneed his horse toward the ranch house ahead.

Holland's gut convulsed as Print Olive stepped onto the porch. There were four other men on the porch, all wearing guns and scowls. Holland wondered if he might be looking at the last thing he would ever see in his life.

"Hello, Del," Print said casually. "Light and set. We've still got some coffee on."

The sheriff cleared his throat nervously. "Print, I've come to arrest you. Got the paper in my pocket here."

Print Olive raised an eyebrow. A half smile flickered across his face. "Arrest me, Del? What for?"

"Two counts of murder. One assault with intent to murder. Sworn out by W. H. McDonald."

Print shook his head. "Too bad. I was hoping the bastard died." He cocked a hip against the porch railing. "Del, you know they were rustlers. I caught them at it."

"You've got to stand trial, Print. I'm sorry, but I'm going to have to take your gun and take you to jail."

Print fixed a steady gaze on the sheriff. "You know I don't give up my gun to anybody. And there's no jury in Williamson

County that will convict mc of killing a cow thief. That's the same as killing a coyote around here."

"Print, I have to—"

"Tell you what, Del." Print stepped from the porch. Holland flinched as the dark-eyed gunman strode forward and stopped at his stirrup. "Why don't you just give me that paper and call it even. You have my word I'll show up for the hearing. And even a trial if it comes to that."

Holland reached into his pocket and produced a document with trembling fingers. "That's"—he cleared his throat again—"fair enough, Print."

Print Olive studied the arrest warrant, then nodded. "Looks to be in order. I'll be there." He folded the warrant and tapped it against his palm. "Nothing to get nervous about, Del. I won't hold it against you personally. It won't come to more than a fart in a whirlwind anyway."

"Print, this may be more trouble than you think. There's a witness. Settler named Sam Collins says he saw the whole thing from a hill not a quarter mile off."

Print's eyes narrowed. "Sam Collins, eh?" Print's face softened after a moment. "Del, will you for Christ's sake relax? I've told you I'll come in. Planned to go to Georgetown anyway. Want to look at that new rifle Winchester's come out with. Come in. Have some coffee."

Georgetown
June 1875

Print Olive pushed his way through the crowd on the courthouse steps. He made no attempt to hide his disgust at the turn of events at the hearing. At the same time, he wasn't particularly worried. The judge had ruled there was sufficient evidence for a trial in the McDonald shootings and set the trial date for January. *Makemson says the only proof they have,* Print thought, *is one witness. That can be fixed easy enough.*

Bob Olive strode at Print's left, Deacon Scruggs at his right. Bob had fleshed out until at age nineteen he was almost as tall as

Print, but leaner. Bob's gaze constantly swept the crowd, alert to any threat, his hand near the grips of the new Colt Single Action Army model forty-five at his hip. Print knew Bob was actually hoping for trouble. He hadn't yet had a chance to use the new pistol on anything except targets. The weapon was a twin to the one Print now carried. He had turned the old Remington percussion job out to pasture in favor of the cartridge pistol. The rimfire Henry with its puny cartridge was a memory now, too, its place taken by a Winchester Model 73, caliber forty-sixty. A rifle that would put a man down and keep him there.

Deacon plodded along in a relaxed gait, his eyes squinted against the glare of the early summer sun. Deacon still carried the old LeMat pistol, but had given up the ancient Springfield rifle for a new Winchester lever action.

The courthouse crowd thinned in a hurry when Print, Bob and Deacon crossed the street to where four other Olive riders, all heavily armed, waited beside a wagon in front of Georgetown's biggest mercantile store. The wagon was laden with goods destined for the Olive ranch.

"What now, boss?" Rob Murday asked.

Print paused long enough to roll and light a smoke, then winked at Murday. "Courtrooms make me awful dry. I'll buy a couple of drinks around before we head back."

"You want me to stay with the wagon?"

"Rob, I don't believe anybody will be stupid enough to steal from the Olives. Come along, boys," he said, "before that courthouse bunch drinks up all the good whiskey."

Print shared a corner table with Bob, Murday and a nearly empty bottle of Old Crow. The other Olive riders leaned against the bar, laughing and joking, keeping the bartender hopping to fill glasses and beer mugs.

"Wonder how Ira's doing with the trail herd?" Murday said. The herd bound for railhead was the first of the season for the Olives. Two more would follow before the lack of grass put an end to the trail season. Murday idly wondered just how much money Print Olive was now worth. It had to be a bundle. A man didn't get that much power without a lot of coin.

"I doubt there's been any trouble," Print answered. "He's got Nigger Jim and Jay along." Print poured another shot of whiskey into his glass. "Speaking of which, we best get back to the ranch and get some work done—while we can all still walk." He sipped at the drink. "Bob, when you finish that drink, fetch our horses from the livery."

Bob upended his glass and drained the contents in two swallows. He rose without speaking and headed for the door. Bob's stride was steady, Print noted. The kid was learning how to hold his liquor. He still got a touch waspy after a few drinks.

Bob had been gone for fifteen minutes when gunshots sounded from the direction of the livery. Print jumped from his chair and sprinted for the door.

A crowd of excited onlookers had already gathered when Print reached the scene outside the stable doors. Bob was working the ejector rod of his Colt, kicking spent cartridge casings into the dust at his feet. Two bodies lay in the street before him. Bob's eyes had a wild look in them. His breathing was shallow and rapid, like a man getting his money's worth from the town whore on a Saturday night.

"What happened, Bob?"

Bob nodded toward the downed men. "These two jumped me. One had a pistol. The other came at me with a singletree."

Print squatted on his heels to examine the bodies. Both the dead men were Negroes. One lay on his back, sightless eyes turned to the sky, two bullet holes in the chest and a Starr conversion pistol at his feet. The second lay on his side, a pulpy mess left where his jaw had been. Blood pulsed through a second bullet hole below his collarbone. He shuddered once and died. A singletree lay at the side of the body.

Bob thumbed fresh cartridges into the Colt and hefted the gun as he spun the cylinder. "Packs a hell of a wallop, Print," he said.

Del Holland pushed through the crowd, breathless from his sprint from the courthouse. He glanced at the dead men in the street, then at Bob. "What happened here?"

Bob repeated his story as he holstered the Colt. Holland glanced at Print, then back at Bob. "I'll have to take your gun, Bob. You're under arrest."

"No need for that, Sheriff," a man in a silk suit and bowler hat said from the edge of the crowd. "I saw the whole thing. It happened just as the young man said. He had no choice but to defend himself. I might add, sir, that that was one fine piece of shooting."

Holland looked toward the speaker and silently breathed a sigh of relief. "Will you sign a statement to that effect, sir?" The man nodded. "Guess that puts an end to it, then. Bob, I'll need a signed statement from you before you leave town. The county will bury these two."

Print took Bob's elbow and led his brother from the scene. He overheard a remark from the crowd as they passed: "Just a couple more uppity Lincoln niggers got tickets to hell from the Olives."

Nobody, Print knew, was going to file charges against Bob. Not over a couple of black men. Print wasn't even sure it was against the law to kill a nigger in Williamson County.

He was sure of one thing, though. Bob Olive enjoyed killing. He had seen it in his eyes.

Kimbro, Williamson County
August 1875

Sam Collins propped his hoe against a pecan tree at the end of a turnrow and reached for the burlap-covered water jug at the base of the tree. He swiped a grimy hand across the sweat that poured down his face and thought there had to be a better way to make a living than fighting weeds in a cotton patch under a broiling summer sun.

He plucked the corncob stopper from the jug and drank thirstily, eyes closed, until his parched mouth cooled. He lowered the jug, opened his eyes—and almost dropped the water container in shock and surprise at the sight of the big black man standing almost within arm's reach.

"What—who are—" Collins sputtered.

"Mister Collins, I don't mean you no harm," the black man said. "My name's Jim Kelly. I ride for Print Olive."

Collins's initial surprise gave way to a growing panic. The

black man carried a big pistol on his hip. "What you want with me?"

Jim Kelly leaned casually against the pecan tree. "Well, Mister Collins, I reckon a lot of that depends on you. Mister Print, he wasn't too happy when you testified against him in them rustler killin's. But he's willin' to let bygones be."

Kelly let his gaze drift around the field of withered cotton stalks. "Been a touch dry lately, ain't it? Bet a man couldn't make five bales out of this field. Sure not much money in farmin'." Kelly reached into a shirt pocket and brought out a handful of bills. "Now, Mister Print don't like to see nobody starve out. His thinkin' is that a man who sudden-like loses his memory deserves a reward."

Kelly thumbed through the bills. "Right smart of money here. Must be nigh onto a hundred dollars. 'Bout a year's worth of bustin' your back on a cotton crop. Now, if you was to forget what you seen, this here money would be yours."

"You're offering me a bribe not to testify against Print Olive?"

Kelly grinned. "Nope. Offerin' you a choice." He held the bills in his left hand and let his right drop to the pistol. "You can make a hundred dollars easy. Or you could get yourself killed, you got too many principles."

Collins swallowed hard. He knew he was a heartbeat away from death. "Memory's fading on me already." He had to force the words through the knot in his throat.

Kelly's grin widened. "I figured you for a right smart man, Mister Collins." He tucked the folded bills into a low fork of the pecan tree's branches. "I reckon I don't have to tell you that a man don't take Mister Print's money and then turn on him. Folks who try that get hurt. Real bad."

Collins nodded. "I understand."

The farmer stood and watched, a chill raising the hairs on his arms despite the heat, as the big black man turned and walked away. A moment later Collins heard the hoofbeats of a horse moving away at an easy trot. He went to the pecan tree, plucked the bills from the fork and counted the money. It was the most he had ever seen at one time.

"Funny thing," he muttered, "I can't seem to recall one single thing about that day . . ."

Georgetown
February 1876

Williamson County Sheriff Del Holland paced the floor of his office and tried to gather his jangled nerves. The county was going to blow at any time, and he was going to be the man in the middle.

Things had been bad enough before Print Olive's trial in the McDonald shooting. The trial had been the biggest farce in the county's history. The farmer who witnessed the shooting testified he had been drunk as a possum that day and now he couldn't remember straight what had happened. The original indictment against Print had disappeared from the courthouse. The second indictment didn't even mention the two dead men, just the wounding of McDonald. In the end, Print paid a dollar fine for simple assault and walked out a free man.

Del Holland should have been pleased with the way things turned out. He wasn't.

In the past few months he hadn't had a full night's sleep. Two settlers on land adjoining Print's lease had disappeared without a trace. The missing men's widows hadn't been gone from the county a week before two of Print's riders filed claims on the land. And everybody seemed to be stealing from everybody else. One of Fred Smith's riders had turned up dead, shot between the shoulder blades. Two men were found hanged not far from where Old Man Pelsworth's wagon pulled in with his buckshot-riddled body on board.

Holland's butt was sore from the long days in the saddle, talking to people who suddenly didn't have a thing to say, looking for leads into missing settlers and back-shot cowboys and people hanged from pecan tree limbs.

And, he knew, it was going to get worse. James Crow, Crow's ex-convict son and Turk Turner had been making some heavy talk against the Olives—at least out of Print's hearing. The same was true of another faction of small ranchers and farmers who called themselves the Regulators and seemed to have no specific leader.

Holland had heard rumors that someone was planning an attack on Print's ranch, and carried the story to Print in person. Print scoffed at the rumors. Del knew Print was arrogant, greedy, confident of his financial and political power and the guns on his payroll, and thought nothing of running roughshod over anybody who stood in his way. Print Olive was as dangerous as a den of rattlers.

Del Holland stopped pacing and stared out the one window of his office. Georgetown was peaceful today. Few people showed on the streets, kept indoors by a raw north wind and the rattle of sleet pellets against windows and doors. When the explosion came, it wouldn't be so quiet. And it wouldn't take much of a spark to touch off Williamson County.

Holland fingered the star pinned to his vest. There was one way out of this with a whole skin, he thought. He unpinned the star and tossed it on the desk.

He could be in Corpus Christi before week's end.

TEN

Pear Valley, Williamson County
March 1876

Print Olive lay belly-down at the edge of a wild blackberry thicket overlooking the broad meadow on the south side of his ranch. The spring sun heated the receiver of the Winchester in his hands.

Fifty yards away, buzzards circled above the fresh carcasses of two Olive cows.

Print's jaws ached from the clench of his teeth and his temples throbbed in a grinding headache.

The waiting was the hardest part.

Bob Olive had found the cows, throats slit and gutted, two hours after daybreak. Now Bob, Print, Jim Kelly and Deacon Scruggs lay concealed in the brush bordering the meadow, awaiting the return of the hiders who had killed the cows. Print's men had their instructions. They were not to shoot to kill, but to wound the thieves when they returned for the spoils.

Print had another fate in mind for the thieves, a fate that would deliver a message to anyone with a yen for Olive beef and hides. It was a message that would be heard through all of Williamson County.

Print slid his thumb to the hammer of the rifle as a wagon pulled by two mules creaked into view at the upper end of the valley. He grunted in satisfaction as he recognized the two men on the wagon—Turk Turner and James Crow. Print fought back the urge to open fire as soon as they were in range. A quick kill was too good for those two . . .

Print felt his heartbeat quicken as Turner pulled the mules to a stop beside one of the downed beeves. The two men dismounted, their rifles still in the wagon. Neither wore handguns. They stood over one carcass, the sun glinting on steel as they paused to whet the heavy-bladed butcher knives in their hands.

Print thumbed the Winchester hammer to full cock, drew in a deep breath and lined the sights on Turner's left leg. He let out the breath and squeezed the trigger. The rifle slammed against his shoulder. Through the powder smoke Print saw Turner spin and fall as the heavy slug ripped through his kneecap. Crow stood frozen in shock and surprise for an instant, then staggered back as another rifle cracked. Crow went down beside his companion.

Print levered a fresh cartridge into the chamber of the Winchester and stood. "Watch 'em, boys!" he called to his men. "One of them might have a belly gun." He strode toward the wounded men, rifle at the ready. Bob, Jim and Deacon emerged from the brush at the same time. The line of Olive riders moved cautiously to the wagon.

Turner and Crow were past putting up any fight. Turner whimpered in agony, eyes closed. Blood poured from his shattered knee. Crow sat up, dazed, a crimson stain spreading across his side.

Print knelt beside Crow. "Crow," he said, his tone cold, "you two have stepped in it this time. Clear up to the hocks." He quickly frisked the two men. Satisfied they had no concealed weapons, Print stood and nodded toward the grim-faced Olive riders. "Boys, you know what to do."

Bob Olive grinned in anticipation as he pulled a skinning knife from the sheath at his belt and knelt beside one of the dead cows. Jim Kelly picked up one of the butcher knives and went to work on the second carcass.

Turk Turner moaned again and opened his eyes. The first thing he saw was Print Olive's face.

"You've killed your last Olive cow, Turner," Print said. He was smiling. "Caught you with your hand in the pie for sure this time."

"Olive—" Turner's voice broke as a new blast of agony twisted his features. "What—you going—to do?"

"You'll see, Turner."

A few minutes later Bob and Jim finished skinning the cows.

The hides, flecked with blood and bits of tallow, lay flesh side up in the sun. Turner and Crow sat propped against a wagon wheel, trussed in ropes. Print grabbed the rope around Crow's chest, yanked him to his feet and dragged him toward one of the spread hides.

"Olive, what—"

"Ever see what happens to green cowhide left in the sun, Crow? It shrinks, slow. I always thought it would make a good, cheap coffin for a cow thief."

Crow's eyes widened in terror. "My God, Olive! You can't—can't do that to a man—it's inhuman! Just shoot us, for Christ's sake—and be done with it!"

Print chuckled. "Now, Mister Crow, somebody's got to be an example to the cow thieves around here. You and old Turk there have earned the honor." He pushed James Crow onto the bloody cowhide. "Tie him in good, Bob. Make sure the Olive brand shows."

Crow's frantic pleas grew more desperate as Bob wrapped the hide tight around his body and bound it firmly into place with strips cut from the green skin. Jim Kelly did the same with Turk Turner. The Olives ignored the men's pleas for mercy. Turner quit begging to curse vehemently before tears of despair and horror poured down his face.

Print stood back to survey his crew's work. The two rustlers were wrapped tight in the green hides. Within minutes the hides would begin to shrink under the sun's heat. By nightfall the hides would be a third smaller than when they were peeled from the cows. By noon the next day, the lives would be squeezed from Turner and Crow.

Muffled cries and whimpers came from beneath the hides. Print touched the brim of his hat in mock salute as the Olive men mounted. "Can't say our association has been pleasurable, Turner. Or you, Crow. But today makes up for it. Let's ride, men. We've got work to do."

Deacon Scruggs turned for a last look as the Olive crew neared the end of the valley. He felt the beads of nervous sweat on his brow. For a moment he thought he was going to be physically sick. What they had just done was worse than any Comanche trick. Two men would die a slow, agonized death by suffocation. The Mexicans had a term for it. The Death of the Skins. Deacon wanted to protest—at least ask Print to shoot the two, let them escape the obscene end that awaited them—but he knew the plea would fall on deaf ears.

Deacon scanned the faces of the men he rode with. Bob Olive's dark eyes glittered in delight as he whistled an off-key hymn. Jim Kelly's features held no expression, no sign of regret or satisfaction.

It was Print Olive's reaction that bothered Deacon the most.

Print was laughing out loud.

Lawrence Chapel
April 1876

Louise Olive forced a smile to hide the sting of hurt in her heart and held her head high as she strode toward the buggy waiting outside the Methodist church.

She had been unprepared for the firestorm of hate that the deaths of Turk Turner and James Crow had ignited. Louise knew it was not the deaths themselves that alienated so many of her former friends. It was the manner of death. The brutality of the act stunned even the most hardened men. It struck terror into the hearts of the wives of Williamson County. Their men could be next.

The shrunken cowhides squeezed Louise as well. She now was all but shunned at the church socials, quilting bees and other events that helped lift the weight of ranch life. She was an Olive.

Louise nodded a greeting to a trim, well-dressed woman visiting with the minister. A cold glare was the only reply. Louise tried to ignore the snub as she reached the buggy where Billy waited, a scowl on his eight-year-old face. Billy had balked at attending church services several months ago. He accompanied his mother only because she let him drive the buggy. On occasion he lost track of time, and she would find him in front of a store window staring at the rifles and pistols on display as if the mercantile were a candy shop.

Billy neither spoke nor helped his mother climb into the

buggy. Before she was completely settled in he tapped the reins and clucked the sorrel mare into motion. Louise checked the urge to rebuke her son for his lack of courtesy. She glanced at the smooth-cheeked youth and saw a miniature Print Olive holding the reins. Billy had the same black eyes, the same dark complexion, the same intensity as Print. He seldom smiled and never played at children's games with others his age. Billy already had added some worry wrinkles to his mother's face.

The boy was as headstrong and impulsive as his father, and from the day he climbed out of diapers Billy had been obsessed with guns. For years he carried a toy pistol Bob had carved from the fork of a cottonwood tree. He threw the toy away after Print let Billy shoot the little twenty-two rimfire revolver Print sometimes carried as a belly gun on his frequent trips to Round Rock and Georgetown. Now, Billy was pushing—and pushing hard— for his own gun.

Billy's obsession with guns had triggered some monumental battles with his mother. Louise had gotten no support from Print during those arguments. Print's only contribution to the conflicts was to tell Billy that he would get his gun as soon as his hands grew big enough to handle one. Louise knew better than to push the dispute with Print. After all these years she still feared his violent temper, especially after he had been drinking. And Print had been punishing the bottle more and more of late.

As the buggy wheeled toward home Louise realized she shared the fears of the other Williamson County wives. An image kept trying to form in her mind—the vision of an eight-year-old boy dead in the dust of a corral, a small bullet-riddled body covered with blood.

The Olive ranch came into view. Louise tried to summon the courage to face what had to be done.

She had to try to convince Print to leave Texas, or at least Williamson County, before there was more bloodshed. If she had to fight Print, she would—to save the lives of her husband and family. The mere thought of the confrontation to come left her palms sweaty.

Round Rock
July 1876

Print Olive sat alone at a corner table in Blakely's Emporium and glowered at the nearly empty whiskey bottle on the stained wood before him. A cold lump of anger sat like a bad meal behind his belt buckle. Beads of sweat speckled his forehead and his cheeks were beginning to feel numb. The whiskey seemed to be hitting him quicker and harder these past few months.

The outrage over the Turner and Crow killings had taken Print by surprise. *What the hell am I supposed to do,* he grumbled in his mind, *let every damn thief in the county help himself to my beef? What do these people expect?*

James Crow's oldest son had been squalling like a panther to anyone who would listen over his old man's death. He was finding more and more people who would listen. And that damned coward Holland. He owed everything to Print. When it looked like the bronc might start bucking he just dumped the star and left the county. Print's enemies hadn't been long to take advantage of Holland's cowardice. The new sheriff was in their pockets, a cold-eyed man named Ragland who carried a Greener ten-gauge double shotgun. Word was that Ragland was a hired gun, a one-time rustler himself, and that he could be bought but not scared. And Ragland had been making talk that he'd bring charges against the Olives in the Turner and Crow killings.

Worse yet, Print had begun to wonder if Del Holland's warning might not have some bite to it. The farmers and ranchers who had opposed the Olives in the past just might find the guts to attack them. *If they do, they'll find themselves in a fight they won't forget,* Print vowed.

Print had surprised Louise when he listened patiently to her fears for the family's safety. He hadn't snapped at her, hadn't told her to tend to woman's business as he had in the past. He merely nodded and agreed to consider moving to greener pastures if things got worse in Williamson County. It was the first time he had really paid attention to what Louise was saying. *Maybe there's more to her than I figured,* he thought.

Print lifted his glass, downed the contents and refilled the squat tumbler. He stared for a moment at the glass, swirling the amber liquid inside. The conversation with Louise had disturbed Print more than he first thought it would. He had to admit to himself that he needed Louise, couldn't begin to imagine life without her. He also felt the first tinge of shame. He hadn't been the world's best husband and father. He hadn't intended to push her into the background of his life. There just hadn't been that much time. *That dog won't hunt, Print,* he chastised himself, *you could have made the time; you just didn't want to.* Print had been faithful to Louise, and not from lack of opportunity. Power and money seemed to bring women out of the walls, many of them ready to lift their skirts at his word. He hadn't given the word. But he hadn't told Louise that he needed her and wanted her. He couldn't bring himself to say it. That was a sign of weakness in a man.

And Billy. Someday, Print knew, he would be old and tired. It would be up to the son to carry on the family name. In the meantime he needed a man's hand to guide him. Print hadn't given it. Now he wondered if it was too late.

Print would be true to his word to Louise. Ira was due back from trailing a herd north any day now. He would talk it over with Ira. Swallow that Print Olive pride if need be. *God,* he mused, *that would be something; Print Olive run out of the county by a bunch of clodhoppers and three-cow ranchers . . .*

He sipped at the drink. His eyes narrowed as the Emporium door swung open. Fred Smith and Cal Nutt stepped into the saloon and strode toward the bar. Fred carried a pistol at his belt. Print had never seen Fred with a handgun before. Cal was never without one.

Print watched as Fred glanced around, saw Print and changed direction. He walked straight to Print's table. Fred's eyes were narrowed, jaws clenched beneath a two-day stubble of beard.

Print nodded a greeting.

Fred ignored the nod. He stood at Print's table and looked down at the bigger man. Print saw the smoldering anger tinged with contempt in Smith's gaze.

"Drink, Fred?"

"Not with you, Print," Fred said. His voice was low, his tone cold. "You've gone too far this time."

Print felt his own anger rise. "Meaning?"

"Turner and Crow. I can't back a man who would do something like that. Don't expect any help from me or my crew in the future."

"I always figured you for somebody who stood behind his friends, Fred. I guess I figured wrong."

"No, Print. I still back my friends. But as of now, I guess you aren't one of them any longer." He turned his back and strode away before Print could reply.

Print glowered at the cattleman's back, rage souring the whiskey in his gut. "I don't need fair-weather friends, Smith," he muttered to himself. "The Olives can take care of themselves." He pushed his chair back and strode toward the door, weaving slightly from the effect of the liquor. He did not look toward Smith or Cal Nutt standing at the bar. *To hell with you, Smith. And with all your kind.* Print shoved through the door into the blast of heat from the raging sun outside.

Lawrence Chapel
August 1876

Bob Olive swabbed the sweat from the back of his neck with his kerchief and glared toward the dancers swirling on the makeshift wooden platform erected near the schoolhouse. He cursed under his breath.

The residents of Lawrence Chapel were always looking for an excuse to hold a big feed and all-night dance. The wedding of one of the Alexander girls provided the reason for this one. Bob paid no attention to the bride, a horse-faced and heavy young woman whose main claim on a man was her father's money. Old man Alexander was one of the few farmers who always seemed to turn a hefty profit from the sandy loam soil of his place just outside of town. He now owned a piece of the bank, part of the livery stable, and several county officials.

Bob hadn't bothered to attend the wedding. It was the dance that held his interest. More specifically it was Carolyn Thurber, a cousin of the bride, that drew him to Lawrence Chapel on a muggy summer night.

Carolyn was tall and sultry, with deep green eyes and a face and figure to make a man snort and paw the ground. And she had spent most of the night in the arms of Cal Nutt.

Bob reached for the flask in his hip pocket and took a hefty swallow of the potent rye whiskey. He grimaced as the liquor sent its fire through his stomach. He never took his eyes from Carolyn and Nutt. Carolyn had her head thrown back, laughing, her pelvis pressed against Cal's hips. *Damn his soul,* Bob fumed silently, *first the bastard and his boss turn their backs on us and now he's trying to steal my girl.*

The fact that Carolyn Thurber wouldn't tell Bob if his pants were on fire had to be Cal Nutt's fault. *Spreading lies about me and Print, that's what he's done. By God, he's going to pay for it before this night's out.*

Bob took another slug from the bottle. He let his hand brush against the little Smith & Wesson Model Three top break thirty-two in his belly band, wishing he had the big Peacemaker instead of the little popgun. It was accepted in Lawrence Chapel that firearms weren't allowed at social functions. Bob ducked that problem with a hideout gun and he was sure at least half the crowd had done the same. The thirty-two had about as much bite as a mosquito. But at close range it would do the job.

"Let's give the band a break, folks," old man Alexander called from the stage. "Everybody have some punch, cool off a bit, and we'll be back dancing in fifteen minutes."

The crowd applauded in appreciation as the musicians put down their instruments. Bob knew he was about to get his chance. Whenever Cal Nutt was not in Carolyn's arms, he slipped off to the stable with some of Fred Smith's other hands for a quick lick at the whiskey bottle hidden there.

Bob slipped away from the lanterns lighting the dance floor. He kept to the shadows, working his way toward the livery stable. He paused at the side of the stable door to listen. Nutt and another man were laughing and joking inside. Bob stepped through the door and eased the thirty-two from his waistband.

Cal Nutt stood in a corner of the barn, relieving himself against the wall. His companion, another Smith rider, lounged on a hay bale.

Bob lifted the pistol. "Nutt, you sonofabitch," he yelled, "you've just pissed your last piss!"

Nutt spun, startled. Urine sprayed as Bob cocked the little thirty-two. His finger tightened on the trigger.

A bone-jarring blow slammed into Bob's gun arm, sent the pistol spinning away. He cried out in pain as he saw a third Smith rider at his side, an axe handle in his hand. He hadn't known the man was there. Bob fell to his knees, clutching his battered gun arm against his ribs, almost paralyzed in pain.

The axe handle walloped into his shoulder, knocking him prone. The man with the hickory shaft raised it above Bob, ready to crush his skull.

"Hold it, Jake!"

Cal Nutt's yell stayed the man's swing. Bob looked up through tears of pain as Nutt buttoned his pants and strode toward him. "I'll take care of him."

Nutt kicked Bob in the side of the head. Hands yanked Bob to his feet. Nutt swung a fist into Bob's face. Bob saw the blood and sweat spray and realized it was his own. Cal Nutt's fist came at him again. The light from the stable lantern faded to red and winked out.

ELEVEN

Olive Ranch
August 1876

Bob Olive eased his aching body into his bedroll fifty yards from the bawling herd of longhorns in the big corral and tried to find some part of his anatomy that functioned without pain.

The beating at the hands of Cal Nutt and the two Smith riders had left its lingering stamp. His bruised and battered head still ached. His breath whistled through a broken nose. The cut over his eyebrow stung from sweat beneath the bandage, and every time he breathed it felt as if someone had rammed an ice pick into his side. He was sure he had a cracked rib. His right arm was a bluish-purple from elbow to wrist. At least the axe handle hadn't broken any bones. He could still use a gun. *And right now,* he thought bitterly, *there's one man I'd sure as hell like to have in my sights. Cal Nutt.*

He hadn't been exactly overloaded with sympathy from Print after the fight. "Little brother," Print had growled, "how many times do I have to tell you not to just barrel into a fight without knowing the odds? You're just plain stump-dumb lucky you didn't get killed." Not so much as a how do you feel, are you hurt bad—just a butt-chewing. Print had shown him no mercy during the cattle gather today. Bob didn't expect any tomorrow when the branding began. He groaned at the thought of the day's work to come. Two hundred cattle, most of them nearly full grown, to be roped, wrestled, branded and the bulls castrated. It was going to be a long day.

Bob ran his tongue over the cuts inside his mouth and winced at the coppery taste of tender flesh beginning to heal. He wanted a stiff belt of Print's good Kentucky bourbon to ease the pain, but even Print wasn't drinking this week.

Bob had struggled out of his boots in the fading light of day but otherwise lay fully clothed, his Winchester at his side and his Colt and gunbelt draped over the horn of the saddle he used as a pillow. The lowing and clashing of horns from the penned cattle wrecked the peace of the hot August night. Bob was bone-tired and sore, and there were lumps in the ground beneath his roll.

He glanced toward the darkened ranch house nearby, longing for the comfort of his own soft bed. The whole thing seemed stupid, camping out on the grounds when comfort was so close, but it was Print's idea. There had been more talk that a raid on the Olive ranch was being planned. This time Print had taken the rumors seriously. *Print's running spooked,* Bob thought. *I've never seen him run spooked before.*

Print had taken the precaution of moving Louise, the baby, Anna Maria and their most valuable furnishings to Jim Olive's house in Lawrence Chapel. He had also sent four Olive riders, seasoned gunmen, with Louise. *What the hell,* Bob grumbled inwardly, *there have been rumors before, more of them than a man can count, and nothing's ever happened.*

Bob sighed and stared toward the heavens. Low, broken clouds scudded across the sky. The air seemed wet enough that a man could squeeze a handful of it and have enough to drink. A faint quarter moon played tag with the clouds. It was going to be dark as sin when he had to roll out of his blankets at three o'clock to stand watch.

He rolled onto his side, trying to get comfortable, and saw Jim Kelly pick up his rifle, pause to speak with Print, then stride away to take the first watch. Print would sleep little tonight, Bob knew. He closed his eyes and drifted into the hazy half-world that came before sleep.

Twenty yards away Print Olive stood and surveyed his defenses once more. He had the best gunhands available on his line. Deacon Scruggs, Jay, Ira, Bob, Jim Kelly and the waspy little black gunman called Bigun because he stood barely five foot two in his boots. Two Mexicans who were adept with riatas and cattle and even better with short guns. Young Silas Morgan, barely thirteen, who knew nothing about cattle but who could nail a squirrel in the head at seventy yards with his little thirty-two-twenty carbine.

Print was satisfied with his plan. He had analyzed the situation as though he were the man planning the raid. They would hit hard and fast, guerrilla-style. Set fire to the house and outbuildings, then pick off the Olive riders as they fled the burning structures, outlined against the flames. They wouldn't be expecting a defensive perimeter. Print's men had adequate cover along the creek that ran past the corrals, in the lumpy mounds of sandy soil and in the clumps of brush that fringed the house and barn.

Print rolled and fired a cigarette. It would be his last of the day. The flare of a match could give away the element of surprise. He dragged the heavy smoke into his lungs. He was sure Louise and Billy would be safe with Jim Olive. The presence of the four Olive gunmen he had sent with them helped ensure that. And his father still had the respect of most of Williamson County. No one would risk an attack on Jim Olive's home. It was Print they wanted.

Print felt the familiar prickle of hairs at the back of his neck, the anxious squirm of his gut. The sensations were bred of instinct during the war, and they always came before an attack. Print had known when a charge was coming before the pickets and generals did.

He dropped the cigarette butt into the dirt and ground it into the soil with his heel. He glanced up as Deacon Scruggs strode to his side.

"You feel it, too, Print?" Deacon's gaze swept the horizon in the last of the fading light.

"I feel it. They're close."

"I reckon we're ready." Deacon levered a cartridge into the chamber of his rifle and strode away.

Print heard Jay's gusty laugh over the bawling of cattle and clash of horns at the corral. Jay was joshing Bigun as he stripped off his shirt to prepare for bed. Jay was the only man in the crew who went to bed shirtless. He had always been hot-natured and couldn't sleep unless he could feel the movement of air over his body on a hot night.

Print watched and waited until the last of the men had bedded

down. The cattle gradually stopped lowing and pushing and settled in for their own rest. A lazy breeze blunted the edge of the
heavy heat. Overhead the clouds were breaking up. The night
would be hazy with only a sliver of moon for light. A coyote
yelped in the distance. An owl sailed on silent wings against the
thin salmon sky, stalking a meal in the meadows below.

For the third time that night, Print Olive checked the loads in
his Winchester and the Colt Peacemaker. The shell belt for the
handgun was full. Print's shirt pockets bulged with extra cartridges for the Winchester and another full box lay at the head
of his bedroll.

Print sank back on his blankets, leaned against the saddle, and
stared into the distance. "All right, you bastards," he muttered
softly, "whoever you are, come on."

The raiders hit an hour after midnight.

A rattle of gunfire jolted Print from his blankets. He scooped
up his Winchester and pistol belt as the clatter of horses' hooves
pounded past the main house and rumbled toward the corrals.
Print glimpsed the flicker of torches at the house as he strapped
on the gun belt and cocked the Winchester.

He slapped a shot toward a mounted man and knew he had
missed. A slug buzzed past his head, another kicked dirt at his
feet. Print fired again and grunted in satisfaction as a horse
stumbled and went down, throwing its rider.

Other Olive guns came into play, the sharp crack of Winches-
ters and flatter blast of handguns ripping the heavy air, answer-
ing the gunfire of the raiders. *Must be fifteen or more of them,* Print
thought. He stood his ground, levered three more rounds toward the approaching line of horsemen, then dived for cover
behind a low mound of earth. The horsemen scattered, their
frontal charge abandoned. Yells of surprise and pain mixed with
the thunder of guns and panicked bawling of cattle. Dust and
powder smoke obscured the faint haze of light from the moon.

A few yards to his left Print saw the shadowy form of Deacon
Scruggs leaning on one knee, his ancient LeMat belching its
unique muzzle flash. A horseman thundered past, almost running Print to the ground. Print fired at the man's back. He
thought the rider flinched, but couldn't be sure of a hit. Shoot-

ing at night was more luck than skill, especially at running targets.

He chanced a glance over the top of the mound. Flames licked at the house and barn. The burning buildings cast a pale red-gold glow. One horseman was outlined against the flames for a few seconds. Print aimed as best he could and squeezed the trigger. Through the bright flash of the muzzle blast Print saw the man tumble from his horse. A second man skidded his mount to a stop as the downed rider stumbled to his feet. Print fired again and missed. The downed man swung up behind his companion and the two vanished into the darkness.

The panic-stricken cattle surged against the corral fence. A section of rails cracked and splintered. The cattle boiled through the opening and surged from the corral onto the prairie.

Print thumbed cartridges into his rifle. Flames from the burning buildings cast a stronger light now. He heard the deep thump of a big-bore shotgun and heard Jay cry out. Print's heart skidded as he saw Jay's shirtless figure stumble backward and go down.

Across a bare patch of ground illuminated by firelight two horsemen bore down on Ira, firing handguns. Print leapt to his feet, levered three quick shots toward the riders and saw them veer aside. Then a heavy fist slammed into his left hip. The impact spun Print around, spilling him to earth as the rifle fell from his grip. For an instant he wondered about the taste in his mouth. He fought against the darkness that tried to enfold him. He realized that the taste in his mouth was sand.

Print pulled the Colt and twisted onto his side as the first wave of pain exploded in his hip. He dragged himself behind a low mound of earth, tried to ignore the agony building in his hip and looked around for a target.

There was none to be seen. A sudden stillness broken only by the crackle of burning buildings fell over the battleground. The attackers had fled.

Print lowered the Colt, his arms and shoulders suddenly losing their strength. He blinked back the darkness again. A bulky form loomed at his side.

"Print? You hit?" Deacon Scruggs stood over Print, thumbing cartridges into the loading port of a Winchester.

"Hip," Print said, his voice faint. "Jay?"

Deacon shook his head. "He's hit hard. Buckshot load in the belly. I don't think he's going to make it."

Rage, physical pain and an almost overwhelming sense of loss knotted Print's throat. "The others?"

"Bigun's dead. One of the Mexicans is down, hit in the chest. Nigger Jim got a bullet burn on a shoulder. Nobody else hurt, far as I can tell." Deacon's big hand eased the Colt from Print's numb fingers. "Lay still, Print. I've sent for a wagon. We'll get you and Jay to a doctor."

Print clutched a handful of Deacon's shirt sleeve. His grip was weak. "Somebody's going to pay for this, Deacon. Somebody's going to pay for Jay—" Print gasped as a new blast of agony ripped through his hip. A red film edged in black obscured his vision. The darkness spread, squeezed the red film into a small dot. The red pinpoint winked out.

Print came awake slowly, groggy. It was as if someone were twisting an auger through his hip.

He opened his eyes, blinked against the glare of sunlight through a window and tried to focus his gaze. He lay disoriented for a moment, then realized he was in his old room at his father's house in Lawrence Chapel.

A slender hand wiped a damp rag across his forehead.

"Louise?"

"I'm here, Print." Gentle fingers traced a path along his throbbing temple.

"How's—Jay?"

He knew the answer by the sudden pool of tears in Louise's eyes. "We're going to lose him, Print. The doctor says there's not a—not a chance—" Her voice broke into soft sobs. Print found the strength to pull her to him. Her hair brushed his cheek.

"I should have listened to you, Louise," he said. "We should have pulled out before—before this happened." He groaned aloud as the auger drove deeper into his hip joint. "Now, I can't leave. Not until I find the man who shot Jay. Then I promise you we'll go. Leave Texas."

The door creaked open before Louise could reply. Bob strode into the room, his face drawn into an angry scowl. "I found out who one of those bastards was, Print," Bob said. He reached into a pocket. "I found this between the house and the corral." He dropped a metal object into Print's palm. "Recognize that?"

Print stared at the watch in his hand. It was a trainman's-style timepiece. The head of a deer was carved into the gold case. His hand closed around the watch. "Cal Nutt. He was carrying a watch like this up in Ellsworth."

"I don't know anybody else around here has one like it." Bob's voice was cold and hard. "If Cal Nutt can't tell us what time it is, Print, the sonofabitch is mine. I owe him."

Print dropped the watch onto the sweat-soaked sheet at his side. "If Cal was there, Fred Smith must have been. Bob, I'm going to ask a favor of you." The effort of talking drained what little strength he had. He could barely hear his own voice. "Don't do anything yet. Wait until I get back on my feet. Then we'll go after them together."

Georgetown
November 1876

Williamson County Sheriff C. J. Ragland stood on the court-house steps, his ten-gauge Greener shotgun cradled in the crook of an arm, and watched Print Olive dismount stiffly from the buggy.

It was the final day of testimony in Print Olive's trial for the murders of Turk Turner and James Crow. A verdict was expected soon and Williamson County loyalties were divided as they never had been before. So far, Ragland had been able to avoid bloodshed. He wasn't sure how much longer he could say that. He just hoped his deadline decree would hold.

Deadline was Georgetown's main street. On one side, more than thirty heavily armed men—riders for the Olive and Snyder ranches, mostly—waited. On the other side at least that many more armed men camped. They were enemies of the Olives, grangers and small ranchers. Rumors were that if Print Olive were found guilty his friends and hired guns would storm the jail and free him. If he were found innocent, the other group stood ready for a lynching party.

Ragland didn't personally give a rip how the trial turned out. Either way, he figured, it was a wash. Turk Turner had been an out-and-out cow thief and nobody could question he deserved what he got, even if they did raise sand about the way he died. James Crow was a decent enough man. But Crow had thrown in with Turner, and he *was* guilty as sin when it came to the Turner ring's rustling. At the same time, if Print Olive were convicted it wouldn't hurt Ragland's feelings a bit. Olive probably deserved a good hanging as much as any man in the county.

But Ragland wasn't going to step aside and let a war wreck his town after the verdict came in. He owed his political allegiance to the coalition of grangers and small ranchers who had gotten him this job, but he wouldn't stand aside for them any more than he would for the Olive bunch. Ragland liked being on the right side of that sheriff's badge for a change. He took this job seriously.

The group that had put him in office had been more than a little surprised, not to mention disgusted, at Ragland's deadline decree and warning that any man who crossed it to start trouble would catch a load of double-ought buck. The Olive group hadn't been surprised. They had, in fact, been rather reasonable about it. They had agreed not to cross the deadline during the trial. They had pointedly made no promises beyond that.

The sheriff nodded a greeting and stepped aside as Print Olive limped painfully past. Olive returned the nod. He looked confident, Ragland thought. There was an arrogance about him that showed through the limp and the pain. The sheriff idly wondered how much money Print and his lawyer had spent to load this jury in their favor. *He should have saved the money,* Ragland thought. *No jury in Williamson County will convict somebody of killing a cow thief. Not even if that somebody is Print Olive.*

C. J. Ragland strode to the hitchrail and swung aboard his sorrel to start his deadline patrol. He rode erect in the saddle, the Greener double in plain view, between two lines of grim-faced men.

Inside the courthouse, Print Olive knew the routine. He handed his pistol belt to the bailiff, a stooped old man who once had been one of the top bronc stompers in Texas before the falls, kicks, bites, broken bones and passing years led him to seek another line of work.

The bailiff grinned at Print. "Olive," he said, "it's gettin' to where you're spendin' more time in this here court than I am." He turned to hang the gun belt on a nearby rack of pegs.

"Keep that Colt close by, Shorty," Print said. "I expect I'll be back for it soon."

The jury retired for deliberations at eleven. By noon the verdict was in—not guilty—and Print Olive was back in his buggy, a free man.

Print settled his aching hip onto the seat and half smiled at Ira, who held the reins. "I sure would like to celebrate," Print said. He glanced toward the cluster of grangers and heard the angry mutter from the crowd. "But under the circumstances, maybe we'd best just go home."

Ira clucked the buggy mare into motion. The Olive hands fell in behind the buggy, riding two abreast.

Print tried to ignore the pain that jabbed at his hip when the buggy jostled over a rock or rut. It would be good to get back home. His men had rebuilt most of the ranch and corrals while Print was laid up with the hip. Tomorrow the hands would start the fall gather under Ira's supervision. By late spring next year, they would have one of the biggest herds ever assembled in Central Texas. And if the herd happened to pick up a few stray milk cows or steers from the plow-pushers along the way, so much the better. It would be a payback of sorts for the loss of the house.

The loss of a brother was a different matter. There was still a hand to be played out in that.

When all the cards were on the table, the Olives would pack up, lock, stock and musket, and leave Williamson County. Ira said there was good land for the taking in Nebraska. And there weren't so damn many dirt farmers there. *Let these clodhoppers think they've pushed us out,* Print thought; *when this is over I'll have more cattle and land and money than I could ever get in Texas.* In the meantime, he reminded himself, there was one little problem.

Staying alive.

Print Olive was getting damn tired of stopping lead.

TWELVE

Brushy Creek
January 1877

Sheriff C. J. Ragland pulled his heavy wool coat tighter against the icy north wind and stared at the body in the timber.

The dead man's shirt had been stripped away, the frayed suspenders of his grimy overalls twisted over broad hips. The wide torso had been exploded into a mass of gore by what appeared to be at least two buckshot loads—maybe more—from a big-bore shotgun. A pair of farmer's brogans lay beside the body. *It's like what happened to Jay Olive,* Ragland thought. *Like a man shotgunned as he climbed out of bed.*

He knew the dead man. Klaus Muehler, the big, powerful blond German who had helped organize one of at least three known granger groups opposing the Olives. Rumor had it that Muehler was one of the men involved in the raid on Print Olive's ranch. Ragland didn't put much stock in the story. At least three so-called vigilante organizations had claimed responsibility for the raid, including old man Crow's eldest son. Ragland hadn't been able to find any proof to back up the boasts. He still didn't know who had organized the raid any more than he could prove who killed Klaus Muehler.

The sheriff sighed and motioned to the pale-faced youth who had found the body while hunting squirrels in the heavy timber along the creek.

"Bring the wagon up, Ted. We'll haul him to town."

Ragland was sweating from exertion by the time they had wrapped the big body in canvas and wrestled it into the wagon. He mounted his sorrel, waited for the youth to climb onto the wagon seat, then kneed his mount toward Georgetown. He slipped the tie-down thong from the hammer of the Colt in its holster and pulled his rifle from the boot.

Williamson County, he thought, was getting to look like Gettysburg. This was the fifth body found in the last month. Two men hanged from a pecan tree near the county line, with money still in their pockets. An Olive cowboy shot in the back and killed while riding the north range. One of Fred Smith's riders riddled with bullets along a road three miles from Round Rock.

The killings bothered Ragland less than the stock mutilations. The Olives had lost a dozen prized horses, stallions with testicles shattered by birdshot, mares with teats hacked off and sharpened sticks the size of a man's wrist rammed into their vaginas. Not even Print Olive knew how many cattle he had lost to the hocking knives and small-caliber bullets fired into the gut. Worst of all, to the sheriff's thinking, was the baby calves dead of starvation, their tongues slit so they couldn't nurse. And their mothers bawling in agony as milk caked in their swollen, unsuckled udders.

Dammit, Ragland thought, *it's one thing to kill a man. A lot of those who've died in this county deserved it. But only the lowest form of bastard would torture livestock like that. If I find who's doing it, I'll kill the sonofabitch myself.*

Olive Ranch
February 1877

Louise Olive placed a hand on her husband's forearm, feeling the chill of fear and dread in her own fingers. Print's horse snorted and pawed the ground outside.

"Please, Print," Louise begged, "don't go. It's too soon for you to be riding again—"

"I'll be all right, Louise," Print said. "The hip's better, and the sorrel's got a nice, easy gait."

"But Print, you promised! You said we'd move to Nebraska, away from all this killing!"

Print lifted her hand from his arm none too gently. Anger glittered in his dark eyes. "For Christ's sake, woman! How many times do I have to tell you we can't go anywhere until spring. And I'm not about to leave until Jay's killer has paid for it, if it takes all year!"

Print turned his back on Louise, paused to strap his gun belt around his hips and yank a mackinaw from a peg, then slammed the door behind him. A stab of pain from his hip cut into his rage as he climbed into the saddle. He winced, settled into the hard leather and glanced at the rider waiting alongside. Bob Olive's eyes were as cold and hard as Print's own. "Ready, Bob?"

Bob's hand brushed the Colt at his side. "I'm ready."

"Let's go. It's time to stomp a couple of snakes."

San Gabriel River

Print Olive loosened the Peacemaker at his belt and watched as the wagon rounded a bend in the road. At his back the San Gabriel gurgled toward the Texas Gulf Coast. The wind rustled the leaves of evergreens and rattled the bare branches of cotton-wood, pecan and walnut trees.

The hunt had taken half a day. Now the prey was in sight.

Print reined the sorrel into a stand of pines at the side of the road and waited patiently. He and Bob had watched from a distant hilltop as Fred Smith, Cal Nutt and three other riders had left the ranch at dawn. The three riders had headed for the southern end of the Smith range. The Olive brothers ignored them. Cal rode toward Lawrence Chapel. A few minutes later, Bob followed. Print waited as Smith hitched his team and pointed them toward the San Gabriel crossing and the small settlement that lay beyond its namesake river.

It was working out better than Print had hoped. Nutt and Smith riding alone, two Olive men on their trail. He wondered idly how Bob was making out with Cal.

Print dropped his right hand to the butt of the Colt as the creak of wagon wheels drew near. He kneed his horse from the pines and into the center of the road.

Fred Smith had his head down, fiddling with something in the wagon boot. The wagon was within five paces before Smith looked up. He started at the sight of the man on horseback and yanked at the reins. A shotgun clattered against the footboard of the wagon as the team came to an abrupt stop.

"Hello, Fred," Print said, his voice calm despite the cold rage in his gut.

Smith stared in silence at Print for a moment. His eyes widened in surprise and growing fear.

"I never figured you for a snake, Fred," Print said. "But Jay died from your poison. Now it's time to balance things out."

Confusion flickered over Fred Smith's face. "I don't know what you're talking about, Print."

"I'm talking about that raid on my place. Jay was a long time dying."

"Print, I didn't have a thing to do with that," Smith said. "We've had our differences, but I'd never be part of something like that! You've got to believe me!"

Print snorted in disgust. He kneed the sorrel into a quarter turn to his left, opening his gun arm to the wagon. No horse liked the concussion of a gunshot fired almost in his ear. "That's bullshit, Fred. Bob found Cal Nutt's watch by the house you burned. Everybody knows Cal won't so much as take a piss without your saying it's time."

"Print, for God's sake—"

"Shut up, Fred. Because you used to be my friend, I'm going to give you a better chance than you gave Jay. Pull some steel."

"No, Print—you can't force me to draw on you! You'll kill me for sure!"

Print glared at the smaller man on the wagon seat. "You got that right, Fred. One way or the other, I'm going to kill you. You can take it with a gun in your hand or setting on your butt. It makes no difference to me."

Fred Smith's pale face twitched. His hand stabbed for the shotgun beside him. Print whipped the Colt from his holster and fired. The slug caught Smith high in the chest. The shotgun slipped from his grasp under the impact. Print thumbed the hammer and fired again. The second slug lifted Smith to his tiptoes and tumbled him over the side of the wagon. Print's horse danced aside as the driverless team panicked and bolted past, the wagon sliding and bouncing on the rough road.

Print cocked the handgun again, waited for the dust to settle, then rode to the fallen man. Fred Smith lay on his back, blood pouring from the double wounds in his breast. Smith tried to raise himself on his elbows, coughed and fell back into the dirt. Print lifted the Colt and sent a third slug into Smith's forehead.

Print sighed in satisfaction as he reloaded the Colt. He holstered the gun and smiled down at the dead man. "Have a good time in hell, Fred," he said softly. He took the lariat from its tie strap, shook out a loop and dropped it over the dead man's feet. He reined the sorrel toward the San Gabriel a few yards away, dragging the body.

Twenty minutes later the remains of Fred Smith sank into a deep pool in a cut along the bank of the San Gabriel, weighted with two heavy, flat stones.

Print dusted his hands, ignoring the pain the exertion had triggered in his hip, and mounted. He glanced at the cold late winter sun halfway down its western slide.

"You can rest easy now, Jay," he said softly. "I know for sure that I will." He reined the horse toward home.

Lawrence Chapel

Bob Olive checked his leggy bay half a block from the Buckhorn Saloon and stared toward the hitchrail in front of the newest structure in the growing community of Lawrence Chapel. Cal Nutt's dappled gray stood hipshot at the rail.

Bob ignored the bite of the wind as he shucked his long coat and draped it across the saddle horn. The wind rippled the leather vest that hung unbuttoned across his chest. He didn't feel the cold as he slipped the hammer tie down from his pistol and put the bay into motion with a gentle touch of the spurs.

He studied the street as he rode, aware of the hard glares from the farmers and other men lounging on the street and peering through windows and doors. Lawrence Chapel today was full of men who hated the Olives. He wondered for an instant if he would be able to ride out alive, then shrugged away the thought as he stepped from the saddle in front of the Buckhorn and tossed the reins loosely across the hitching rail.

Bob stood outside the door for a moment, curbing the impulse to charge in with the pistol blazing. The important thing now was that Cal Nutt looked into the eyes of the man who was going to kill him.

He toed open the saloon door and stepped inside, a calm deliberation shoving aside the embers of rage. He stood quietly for a few seconds to allow his vision to adjust to the poor light in the saloon. A massive rack of whitetail deer antlers stood prominently above the mirrored backbar. The antlers gave the place its name. The smoky drinking establishment was crowded with merchants, farmers, ranchers and cowboys. It took a few seconds for Bob to spot Cal Nutt, leaning against the bar. Nutt's back was to the door. He laughed at something the swarthy man at his side said.

Alright, Bob told himself, *play it smart; make a wrong move in here and you're a dead man.* He strode to the bar and squeezed into a space three drinkers away from Nutt. Moses Archibald, owner and sole bartender of the Buckhorn, turned a weary glance toward the newcomer. Moses's eyes widened as he recognized Bob.

"Whiskey," Bob said. "Old Crow. Not that sheepdip you keep as bar stock."

The man at Bob's side glanced at him, then drew warily away from the bar. It was no secret around Williamson County that Bob Olive had sworn to kill Cal Nutt; the man wasn't particularly eager to get caught in a crossfire.

Moses Archibald's fingers trembled as he poured a shot for Bob. "Mister Olive, I don't want any trouble in here," he said, almost pleading.

Bob fixed a hard glare on the whiskey peddler's face. "Can't promise there won't be any." He tossed back the bourbon at a gulp and put a quarter on the counter. Cal Nutt still had his back turned to Bob, yarning with the man at his right. Bob slipped the gold watch from the pocket of his vest.

A hush fell over the Buckhorn as awareness spread through the crowd. Men sidled from the bar or moved away from tables.

"Hey, Cal," Bob called, "you got the time?"

Nutt stiffened at the sound of Bob's voice, then slowly turned. The man at Nutt's side scrambled clear of the line of fire. He tipped over a beer stein in his haste.

"What did you say, Olive?" Nutt's blue eyes narrowed. His right hand dropped to his belt. He had a revolver tucked into his waistband.

"I asked you what time it was." Bob flicked his wrist and sent the timepiece skidding down the smooth wood of the bar. "I've been keeping it wound ever since I found it. Close to where Jay was shot."

"I don't know what the hell you're talking about, Olive. I lost that watch in a poker game a year ago."

Bob raised an eyebrow. "Sure you did, Nutt. And a cow's got wings." The tension lay heavy in the Buckhorn. At the corner of his vision Bob saw Moses Archibald edge toward the cashbox. "Stay away from the scattergun, Moses," Bob snapped. "This is between Nutt and me. No reason for you to get hurt."

Nutt's hand crept closer to the butt of the pistol. "You got it wrong, Olive. But, by God, you want trouble, I'll oblige." He yanked at the handgun.

Bob drew his Colt and thumbed back the hammer. Nutt was a shade faster. His pistol thundered and Bob felt the tug of a bullet at his vest. Bob took his time, centered the muzzle and pulled the trigger. Nutt staggered back two steps and tried to raise his pistol. Bob shot him again. Nutt grunted, spun and fell face down.

Bob cocked the weapon again. He waved it from side to side as he backed toward the door. No one moved to stop him. He shoved through the door, took two quick steps, swept the reins into his hand and was in the saddle before the first yell went up from the Buckhorn. Bob holstered the Colt, whipped out his belt knife and sliced the reins of the horses tethered to the hitch rail. He again pulled his gun and fired a shot into the air. The horses, already walleyed in fright from the gunfire inside, scattered on the run.

Bob heard shouts from the Buckhorn as he spurred the bay: "Get the horses! Bring a rope! He killed Cal!"

A pistol ball hummed past Bob's head. He twisted in the saddle, threw two quick shots toward the door of the saloon and heard a startled yelp. Then he was clear of the main street, spurring hard toward the Olive ranch on a leggy bay bred for speed.

Bob brought the exhausted horse to a stop in front of the ranch house. Ira waited, drawn by the sound of hooves.

"What happened, Bob?"

"I killed that bastard Nutt." Bob swung from the bay and reached for the saddle cinch. "They'll be after me, Ira. It was a fair fight. He got off the first shot. Punched a hole in my vest. But there's lynch talk—"

Ira sprinted to the edge of the house, yelled for a fresh horse, then turned to Bob. "You've got to get out of here, Bob. Out of Texas. Print can't bail you out of this one. It's no time for an Olive to be looking at a jury, let alone a lynch mob."

Ira led Bob inside and yelled for Anna Maria to throw some grub in a sack. A query in Spanish came from the kitchen. "No time to explain now, Anna Maria—just do it," Ira snapped. He strode to Print's desk in the corner of the room, grabbed a handful of bills from a drawer and handed them to Bob. "Head for Wyoming. Stay away from big towns. There could be flyers out on you soon. There's a federal judge named Carey owns a ranch north of Cheyenne. Tell him you're a friend of Dudley Snyder. Take the name of Stevens. We'll get word to you when we hit Nebraska."

Rob Murday had Bob's saddle on a rangy buckskin by the time Bob emerged from the house. Ira strapped saddle bags stuffed with food and ammunition into place as Bob mounted. Ten minutes later Bob Olive was a speck in the distance, riding hard toward the northwest.

Olive Ranch

C. J. Ragland nodded a greeting. Print Olive leaned against a fire-scarred porch post, a Winchester in his right hand. The sheriff feared no man, but his gut twitched a bit as he dismounted and looped the reins over the hitching rail. In this part of the world it was still socially acceptable to shoot the messenger sometimes.

Ragland stopped with his left foot on the first step of the porch, rolled a smoke and tossed the makings to Print.

"What brings you out this way, Sheriff?" Print asked as he fashioned his own cigarette, then flipped the tobacco sack back to Ragland.

"Official business, Print. I've got a warrant for Bob's arrest in the shooting of Cal Nutt."

"Won't do you much good, Ragland." Print paused to strike a match on the porch rail and light the cigarette. "Bob's gone. Left the country."

Ragland nodded. "I expect he had some good advice there. There's a four-hundred-dollar price on his head." Ragland took a drag on his cigarette. Print Olive's expression hadn't changed. *Might as well get both feet wet,* he thought. "Print, I'm also carrying a warrant for you. Suspicion of murder. Fred Smith's disappeared."

Print raised an eyebrow and squinted through the smoke. "That a fact?"

"He hasn't been seen for over a week. His team turned up in San Gabriel. There was blood on the wagon seat. I don't suppose you know what happened?"

Print shrugged. "Can't say as I know. Or even care much." He took another drag on the smoke. "You said you had a warrant?"

Ragland tossed his own cigarette aside and reached beneath his long coat. He produced the paper and handed it to Print. "I'll not try to take you in, Print, if you give me your word you'll show up for the hearing. The date's on the warrant."

Print glanced at the document and tucked it into a shirt pocket. "I'll show, Sheriff. Think you'll have a body by then? Can't prove there's a murder without a body. Could be old Fred just decided to leave the country in a hurry."

"Could be," Ragland agreed, "but there's a lot of hard feelings out there against you Olives. Talk of a mob and lynchings. The courts may have acquitted you and your boys of some killings, but public opinion says you're guilty. Print, I don't think I can keep the lid on this keg much longer by myself. I've written to Austin. I've got to call in the Texas Rangers."

Ragland saw the flicker of interest in Print's dark eyes. Print flipped his cigarette butt away.

"Don't blame you, Sheriff. But there won't be any problem. As soon as I get my stock together, we're heading out. Getting too much law and order around here, too many dirt diggers and three-cow ranchers. Man can't swing a cat around here anymore without somebody gets scratched. We'll be in Nebraska come summer."

Ragland breathed a silent sigh of relief. With the Olives gone and the Texas Rangers on hand, maybe one sheriff would be out of the crossfire. He nodded. "I can't say I'm sorry to hear that. But I wish you well." He unhitched his horse, toed the stirrup and mounted.

"Ragland," Print said, "maybe we've never been exactly friends, but we haven't been enemies either. I'm glad of that. I never said this to another man before, but I don't think I'd want to tangle with you."

"That feeling is mutual, Print." Ragland touched his hat brim in salute. "I'd appreciate it if you would show up for that hearing." He didn't believe it was necessary to add that he would come after Print Olive if he didn't show. Both men understood that.

Print nodded. "I'll be there, Sheriff."

THIRTEEN

North Texas
May 1877

Louise Olive twisted in the buggy seat and craned her neck in hopes of catching a glimpse of Billy, riding somewhere with the men. It didn't seem right that a boy just shy of his tenth birthday should be on the back of a full-grown horse within reach of the needle-sharp points of the longhorns.

But the herd on the trail north was too big and strung out too far to spot one small horseman among more than two dozen adult riders. She had worried constantly about Billy's safety from the time the Olives had left Williamson County. *Lord,* she prayed silently, *please don't let anything happen to him; not now, with a new life ahead.*

Despite her worries over her son Louise still felt a powerful sense of relief at leaving Central Texas and all its woes behind. She had suppressed a shudder as the Olives moved through a virtual gauntlet of solemn men and women who watched from wagon, horseback or afoot as the herd and accompanying wagons pulled away from Lawrence Chapel. She could feel the hate in those silent stares.

Print seemed eager to begin a new life. The charge against him had been dropped. Fred Smith's body had never been found. The Olives were leaving with the legal slate wiped clean in Texas—except for Bob, who now was on the Texas Rangers' list of wanted fugitives. But Bob was beyond reach in Wyoming.

Louise already missed her in-laws. Jim and Julia Olive had chosen to stay behind in Lawrence Chapel, as had Marion. Jay lay dead in the family cemetery. She still mourned Jay, the absence of his ready laugh, his practical jokes, even his teasing. She missed her home, even though it had never been completely rebuilt after the fire, and she knew Print would build another when they settled in Nebraska.

It was, she told herself, an even trade.

In Nebraska her men would be safe from the people who wanted to see them dead or maimed. The dream still haunted her, the vision of Billy's small body lying dead in the dust. In Nebraska, maybe guns wouldn't be such a part of their everyday lives. Maybe then Billy's obsession with firearms would end. And as the son settled down in a new and fresh environment perhaps his father would, too. Away from the torment of Williamson County, maybe Print's violent temper would ease. They could be a couple instead of being just a man and his wife. Maybe begin to really share each other's lives, hopes and dreams. *Maybe,* she thought, *I won't have to be afraid anymore.*

Only a few miles ahead lay the Red River. Texas stopped at the muddy waters. Beyond the twisting stream bed lay Indian Territory, then Dodge City and finally the extension of the Western Trail into Nebraska. And home.

Louise idly wondered if Texas had ever seen such an outward migration. The Olive procession was an impressive one, even to those who rode it. Print rode point, usually with Nigger Jim Kelly at his side, followed by Louise's buggy and a long train of supply wagons carrying everything from nails to flour barrels. At the rear of the supply train were other wagons carrying the families of the cowboys and other ranch workers. The line of wagons was so long that the entire procession was seldom in view.

Deacon Scruggs rode alongside her buggy. The gaze from his one good eye constantly swept the countryside, alert for danger. Louise was grateful for his protection. A lady couldn't ask for a kinder, more polite man—or if the need arose, a more fierce protector—as an escort and bodyguard than the big former Confederate soldier. He also bathed more often than most of the ranch hands.

Some distance from the wagon train the Olive herd moved along at a plodding, grazing pace. Louise had no idea how many cattle they owned, but it was in the thousands. The herd itself strung out over ten to fifteen miles when grass and water were good, more than that when they were scarce. The *remuda* of

Olive horses, several hundred strong and many of them mares in foal or with a colt at side, moved along under the watchful eye of several Mexican wranglers.

Louise couldn't imagine how long it would take the whole of the Olive entourage to move past a given point. She knew only that it would be an impressive amount of time. The string of wagons and livestock was so long that three separate camps were usually needed for the overnight stops.

Some women, she mused, would complain at the discomfort of traveling in such a manner. But she had her own sleeping quarters in the wagon that followed her buggy. The wagon was warm and dry, and with canvas stretched over the bows it kept the elements at bay. The men slept in bedrolls on the ground in fair weather and in tents when the elements turned foul. Louise had Anna Maria Ontiveros to help, more than enough to eat, plenty of clothing and medicines. She knew the sun and wind would emphasize the freckles on her nose and shoulders, but that was of no matter. If there was anything to be said of the memory of true poverty, she thought, it was that it made a trip like this seem almost luxurious.

She turned once more in the buggy seat, searching for her son among the riders in the distance. She didn't see him. She could only hope Billy was in good hands. Someone like Rob Murday, maybe. Since Print had spared his life the onetime rustler had become one of the most loyal Olive employees. He had lately taken Billy under his wing, teaching the boy the intricacies of horsemanship and how to handle cattle. That, Louise thought, was a good thing, because the boy needed a teacher.

Print and Billy did not get along well. The boy was impulsive, headstrong and balky like his father. Print didn't have the patience to teach the boy. Instead of showing him how things were done, he snapped and growled, and even at times cursed Billy's fumbling attempts. Louise believed that deep down the boy wanted to please his father, to earn his praise. But Billy didn't know how to earn it and Print didn't know how to give it. *Maybe in Nebraska,* she thought, *they will learn how to get along.*

To Louise Olive, it seemed that her entire life now boiled down to that one phrase:

Maybe in Nebraska.

Custer County, Nebraska
August 1877

Print Olive pulled his horse to a stop on a low ridge overlooking a wide, sandy valley, free of rocks or timber and dotted with splashes of color from late-blooming red-hipped prairie roses. The short, thick grass was lush and green from summer rains. A clear stream fed by spring water wandered through the valley. The banks of the stream showed no traces of major drought or flood.

And they hadn't seen a cow for miles.

Print dismounted and knelt amid the grass rippling in the gentle east wind. He plucked a stem, crushed the blade between his fingers and sniffed the remnants. It would do. In fact, he thought, this could be the best grass he had ever seen.

He pulled the crude map from his shirt pocket. The old buffalo hunter and ex-army scout down on the Republican River had been right. The open range country was dotted with small gullies and arroyos, fresh water, and could support thousands of cattle in fine style. He glanced at the name lettered on the map.

The Dismal River.

An unlikely name, he mused, for the base range of his cattle empire.

He had held the herd for a while along the Republican River. It had promise. But the range there had been claimed by big and powerful cattlemen, a couple of them backed by European money. They had already bought up the available politicians. Buying them back would be too expensive. A man needed to own a few officials before he could build a ranch as big as the one Print wanted.

The Republican ranchers would fight to hold their winter range. The gunmen on their payrolls were as good as Print's hands. And the Republican was filling up fast with settlers brought in by town developers and the railroads. Many of the settlers already in the region were former buffalo hunters, tough men who were crack shots with those long guns and had guts enough to use them.

Land was scarce along the Republican and Print had no desire to be boxed in. He needed room, a place where he could grow. A place where you could ride for miles and not see a cow that wasn't wearing an Olive brand.

And now he was looking at it.

He glanced at the rider at his side. "This is it, Ira," he said. "Olive range. Home." *And nothing standing in the way but a half-dozen or so settlers without two hundred cows among them all. No problem at all . . .*

Olive Town, Nebraska
Summer 1878

Bob Olive rode confidently down the wide main street of the small town that now unofficially bore his family name.

The settlement of some three hundred had been called Plum Creek after the tributary of the Platte River nearby. The former stage stop had grown after the coming of the Union Pacific. It now boasted a school, two churches, a hotel, a railroad depot that also served as a post office, a saloon, a scattering of stores and a blacksmith shop.

Within a few months after the sprawling Olive herd moved past Plum Creek onto the Dismal River range to the north, Print had changed the name of the town.

He had the right, Bob thought. Print owned most of the town now. On the maps it was still Plum Creek, but a letter addressed to Olive Town got here just as quick.

Print had built sod bunkhouses and a few line shacks on the Dismal River range. Cowboys and line riders were scattered across the ranch itself, while Print had bought the biggest house in Olive Town for himself and Louise. A number of Print's top hands also occupied smaller homes Print had bought or leased in the community. The Union Pacific and the Chicago, Burlington & Quincy railroads had spur lines flanking Print's range holdings. Moving cattle, horses and people wasn't that big a problem.

Bob knew there were some who questioned Print's decision to make his home near the Platte, where there were a number of longtime settlers and a county already organized with elected officials. Nigger Jim Kelly had a ready answer for the questioners. "Hell," he had said, "Print just wants to know that the people he owns come through when he tells 'em to."

The reputation of the Olive clan had followed them from Texas. That reputation made it easier for Print to buy out some settlers whose land he wanted. Those who wouldn't sell soon got the word not to buck the Olives if you wanted to stay alive. The elected officials had come cheap. They had also heard the Texas stories.

Print laid claim to all the Dismal River country and thousands of acres around it until cattle bearing the Olive brand now grazed from the South Loup to Plum Creek. The herds flourished and grew on the rich grass and sweet water.

Only two settlers had shown enough gumption to resist Print's invitation to move on.

Ami Ketchum and his older partner Luther Mitchell stuck with their claim along Clear Creek. Bob suspected they would have to be dug out with a Colt. He looked forward to that project.

Bob liked using a gun, reveled in the feel of power it put in a man's hand. He felt a rush of blood in his own veins when he saw a man's eyes widen in terror before he pulled the trigger. He liked the finality of a well placed shot. And he had his eye on Mitchell's stepdaughter. Tamar Snow was seventeen, and the way she was built would make a man whimper. She was supposed to be Ami Ketchum's fiancée. *Too much woman for a three-cow nester with a lace-drawers name like Ami,* Bob mused; *she'll know soon enough what a real man's like.* Take out Mitchell and Ketchum and there wasn't any reason Bob couldn't claim the girl.

He didn't particularly give a flip how she felt about the idea. He hadn't talked to her about it. He didn't intend to. Just take her. Like he should have taken that bitch Carolyn Thurber after he killed Cal Nutt.

Bob had heard Tamar had a couple of brothers, but he wasn't

worried about them. He patted the Colt on his hip. There was an answer for that. Old Colonel Colt had the answer to a lot of a man's problems.

It was good to be home, Bob thought as he swung from his horse before the one-room saloon. Print's letter and traveling money had reached him last fall. It hadn't taken Bob long to quit the Carey spread. That outfit worked a man too hard and paid him too little.

He looped the reins over the hitchrail and pushed into the saloon. He'd drink a toast to the soon-to-be memories of Luther Mitchell and Ami Ketchum. And another to the slim-waisted, full-bodied girl named Tamar Snow.

To put the cork in the jug, he would be drinking his brother's whiskey. It wouldn't cost him a dime.

FOURTEEN

South Loup River
October 1878

Deacon Scruggs spurred his tiring cowhorse into a run and turned back the last of the steers that had tried to bolt. He eased the snorting longhorn back into the herd.

It had been a near thing. They had almost lost a quarter of the gather. Now the cattle had settled down, at least to the extent a wild Texas-bred longhorn ever settled. The lead steer trotted into the sprawling sod corrals where the Olive stock was held until the short drive to railhead and market.

Deacon glanced toward the two horsemen nearby and frowned. Print Olive was chewing out his son again, as if it were the boy's fault the herd had boogered. He waited until the cottonwood rails that made up the crude gate went into place, then reined his mount toward Print. At the same time Billy whirled his horse and trotted away. The boy's face was flushed and twisted in anger and humiliation. Deacon pulled up beside Print.

"It wasn't Billy's fault, Print," Deacon said. "No cowboy in Texas or Nebraska could have turned that spill. He was in the right place—"

"Dammit, Deacon, you keep your nose out of family business," Print snapped. Fury still burned in Print's black eyes.

Deacon glared back, his own anger on the rise. "Print, you can chew on anybody you want. It's your outfit. But you've been riding Billy too hard. You can't expect a boy his age to know what it took you a lifetime to learn about cattle. He's busted his butt in this roundup. It sure as hell wouldn't curdle your milk to say a kind word to him once in a while."

Deacon didn't wait for a reply. He had said his piece. He kneed his horse back toward the pens.

"Dammit," Deacon muttered to himself, "it's Texas all over again and there's nothing I can do to stop it."

Print Olive should be a satisfied man, Deacon thought. The Olive herds flourished on the rich Nebraska range. Beef prices were way up and Print would make more money off this one gather than he had all the time in Texas. Still, he wasn't happy. Rustlers had pecked away at the Olive herd ever since they'd settled here. Deacon figured it was just part of the cost of raising critters. Print didn't see it that way. He might not shy away from taking a stray cow or six on his own, but he got awful testy when somebody took one of his.

Deacon had helped put a couple of cow thieves under Nebraska soil in the last couple of weeks. All that had done was stir up the few settlers who remained. Once again the signs had gone up: *Anyone caught riding an Olive horse or driving an Olive cow will be shot.*

The worst was still to come, Deacon knew.

Print wanted the Clear Creek land claimed by Ami Ketchum and Luther Mitchell. He might have been willing to do without it, but the Ketchum-Mitchell homestead had turned into a rallying point for settlers up and down Clear Creek and beyond. There the settlers gathered to curse the Olives, maybe plan raids on the stock and try to figure out how to put a checkrein on Print Olive's land grabs. *This whole thing is going to blow soon,* Deacon thought, *and somebody's going to get hurt bad. Worse than just dead.*

Deacon knew who that somebody was going to be.

Louise Olive.

Deacon had seen the contentment and the hope fade from her face almost before the dust had settled on the Olives' new range. Her hopes for a fresh start, away from violence and death, had been badly bent already. Deacon sensed they were about to break. The rock that broke them most likely would be Ketchum and Mitchell.

Print Olive had them marked. And where he chalked, the axe usually cut . . .

Clear Creek Ranch

Luther Mitchell dropped the kingpin through the swivel joint of the wagon tongue and the front axle assembly. He tightened the nut with a heavy spanner and grunted in satisfaction.

He was a slightly built man of middle age, old for the life of a settler in a raw land by some standards, but those who knew Luther Mitchell saw beneath the stooped shoulders and wrinkled skin a man who could still do a solid day's work without breaking too much of a sweat. Still, the ache across his shoulders reminded him the wagon repair was a chore he should have waited for Ami's help on.

Mitchell sucked at a skinned knuckle where the spanner had slipped and stared toward the approaching wagon a mile off along the Clear Creek road. He strode to the solidly built, long double sod house he shared with Ami—half the structure was on Mitchell's claim, the other half on Ketchum's—and plucked his rifle from beside the door. The old Sharps Fifty, now converted to metallic cartridge, had served him well as an army scout. There were more modern guns available, but this one still shot where it pointed.

The wagon drew near enough that he recognized it. Luther lowered the rifle, propped it against the door and waited. The wagon belonged to Samuel Durham, a neighbor from only ten miles off. It was piled high with furniture and other personal items. It looked to Luther like Samuel was pulling out.

He tipped his battered felt hat to the woman on the seat with Samuel as the wagon creaked to a stop in front of the sod house. "Afternoon, Missus Durham, Samuel," he said. "Good to see you folks. Climb down. I'll put coffee on."

Durham shook his head. "We're leaving this country, Luther," he said. "I had some visitors last night. Bob Olive, that big nigger gunman and a half-dozen other Olive hands. Bob did most of the talking. He offered me a deal. Five hundred dollars for my claim or six foot of my own dirt to lay under. I took the money. I can't fight the Olives."

"Now, Samuel," Luther said, "I sure can't tell you what to do. But I can tell you you wouldn't have to fight the Olives alone. There's quite a few of us around here have had it with that pushy Texan—"

"And there's a sight fewer of us now," Durham interrupted. "Wiscombe and Terrell disappeared. Halsell burned out. Donovan found drowned in three feet of water. That's a lot of new widows. My wife won't be the next. There's a time to fight and a time to run. I'm running."

Luther Mitchell sighed. "I'm mighty sorry to see you go, Samuel. We've been friends a long time."

Durham shifted his weight on the wagon seat. He seemed embarrassed by his decision not to stay and fight. "I came by for more than just to say goodbye, Luther," he said. "The Olives are probably coming after you next. You and Ami. I'd suggest you load up before they get here and pull out. This is good land but it isn't worth dyin' for."

Mitchell scratched his jaw beneath the heavy beard. "I appreciate your advice, Samuel, but I reckon I'll stay. Ami and me have been working this place too long to let some Texan run us off without a scrap."

"Luther, you know Print Olive will kill you for half an acre if he wants the grass on it. Word's out he's going to set you up. He got his little brother appointed a stock inspector. That gives them a chance to cause all matter of grief." Durham's tone was near desperation. "All they've got to do is find some Olive stock here, which wouldn't be hard to fix, and they'll hang you to the nearest tree."

Mitchell shrugged. "Olive's already been to see me. Made me the same offer he made you. I told him to go piss on a stump— excuse my language, ma'am—and that I wasn't interested in leaving. Then he told me to keep my cows off his range and he pointed right at the ground I'm standing on when he said it." Mitchell's voice raised in anger. "I got friends, Samuel, a good number of 'em. And I'm not afraid of Olive."

Samuel Durham sighed in resignation. "Nobody ever questioned your guts, Luther, but I'm sorry to hear you say that. They scared the hell out of me. Those Texans are crazy. I hate to think of a friend coming to grief."

Durham picked up the slack in the team's reins, ready to flick the big draft horses into motion. "Talk it over with Ami. You and me are old men, used up, mostly. But Ami and Tamar are young. They can make a fresh start anywhere."

Luther Mitchell extended a hand. "Don't worry about us, Samuel. I'll talk it over with Ami again, but I don't reckon we'll change our minds. Good luck to you and the missus."

"God help you, Luther," Durham said as he released Mitchell's hand. "I fear you'll need all the help you can get." The beaten settler reined his team about, the slump of his shoulders showing his despair.

Luther watched as the wagon jolted away into the distance. He pulled a twist of tobacco from his pocket, gnawed off a hunk and tucked it against his cheek.

"Best keep the old Sharps handy, I reckon," he said to himself. "Somebody sure needs to stand up to those high-handed Olives."

Loup City

Ami Ketchum swung Tamar around the dance floor in a fast waltz, his gaze locked onto the green eyes of the young woman in his arms. He fought back the impulse to pull her to him, bury his face in her sorrel-colored hair, maybe even kiss her right here in plain sight. He chuckled aloud. That would give the fine upstanding folks of Loup City something to talk about. But it might embarrass Tamar. The last thing Ami wanted to do was cause her hurt.

She was a fine figure of a woman. Ami knew it wasn't just prejudice on his part because he loved her. Every whole-bodied man at the Loup City dance watched her move across the dance floor, willowy, fluid, her nose wrinkling the way it did when she smiled or laughed. Some watched with envy and others with outright lust.

Ami didn't care. Tamar was his. They could lust all they wanted. It was his bed she'd be sharing soon.

The music ended with a flourish and was answered by polite

applause from the dancers and scores of bystanders crowded
into the Loup City community hall. The band leader, a longtime
settler with a scraggly beard and a battered fiddle, declared the
musicians would take a short break. Ami held Tamar's elbow
gently as he steered her back to the seat beside her mother.
Luther Mitchell's wife was nearing fifty, but it was obvious where
Tamar had gotten her looks. And she was a good woman, one of
the first to arrive when a settler's child was sick, quick to pitch in
with the cooking at a barn-raising, a comfort to those who had
just buried a loved one. Ami liked her. So did everyone else
along the Loup, it seemed. She would be a fine mother-in-law.

He bowed to Tamar as he deposited her in the chair and made
his way toward the punch bowl. There were two punch bowls.
One was pure punch, for the ladies and the few men who didn't
drink. The other carried a lot more punch than the plain stuff.
It packed a solid wallop and Ami was feeling the hit.

The fiddler stepped up to the long serving table beside Ami
and put a fatherly hand on the young man's shoulder. "Ami,
grab a bottle out from under this table and come with me for a
minute. We need a talk."

The old-timer led Ami from the community hall to a stand of
elms out of earshot from the rest of the crowd, took the bottle
from Ami's hand and lowered the level of the whiskey by better
than an inch.

"What's on your mind, Elmer?" Ami reached for the bottle.

"Ami, you been like my own boy ever since you and Luther
pulled into Clear Creek. I got to tell you, I'm worried. Those
Olives are up to no good."

Ami took a solid pull on the bottle and felt the explosion of
heat when the whiskey hit his belly. "Hell, Elmer, everybody
knows that." He hefted the bottle again. "I guess you're going to
tell me to pull out, too. Seems like that's all I hear these days."

The fiddler sighed. "I know, son. But not everybody under-
stands how dangerous Print Olive is. You ever hear of the 'Death
of the Skins'?"

Ami shook his head.

"Those Olives wrapped two men in green cowhide down in
Texas. Left them out in the sun. Cowhides shrunk and squeezed
'em to death. Awful way to die." Elmer took the bottle and

shoved the cork back into the neck. "It ain't just you I'm worried about, Ami. It's Tamar. That girl couldn't stand it if she lost you, son. It'd put her clean out of her mind." The fiddler reached into his pocket. "I've got a hundred dollars here. It's yours, if you'll get away from here. Go back to Iowa and take Tamar with you."

Ami grinned and shook his head. "I'm not afraid of the Olives, Elmer. I like this country. Tamar and I have our plans already made. There's a valley up on the Rawhide River in Wyoming. I plan to file on it—"

"Then take this money and go to Wyoming. Just leave Nebraska. I don't want to have to bury you."

"No. I won't take handouts. I won't move until I'm ready, when I know I can take care of Tamar the way she deserves." Ami squared his shoulders and smiled. "If the Olives try anything they could find out they've locked horns with a young bull buffalo."

The fiddler sighed. "All right, son. I can't live your life for you." He turned to walk away. "Just remember," he said over his shoulder, "what happened to the buffaloes."

Ami chuckled as he watched the old man go. He had nearly enough money now to file the Wyoming claim. But it would take another year before the Clear Creek ranch earned enough and Ami was an impatient man. He had a plan. It would be a good joke on the Olives when they paid for his claim . . .

Middle Loup River
November 1878

Bob Olive pulled his Winchester from the saddle boot and glared toward the small herd winding its way southward along the river.

He had cut sign on the herd, maybe seventy-five head, a half day back and well into Olive range. Now the stolen cattle were in sight.

Bob's lips twisted in a tight grin as the point rider came into view. Ami Ketchum. *Now I've got you dead to rights, you bastard,* Bob thought, *caught with stolen cattle.* He touched spurs to his bay.

Bob reined in abruptly as he rounded a bend in the rocks and scrub timber along the river. He sat stunned in the saddle. Ami Ketchum stood in the middle of the trail, a Winchester trained on Bob's chest. At Ami's side another rider held a double shotgun. The twin bores looked as big as stovepipes. Bob glanced to his right at the sound of a horseshoe against stone. A third man sat casually in the saddle, a big pistol in his fist.

Bob's surprise faded under a quick push of fear. He hadn't expected to find himself under the gun, and today he rode alone. He knew he could take Ketchum, maybe even the one with the shotgun. But there was no way he could down all three men. The only thing he could do was bluff it out, backed by the knowledge that the whole Olive outfit would ride down anyone who harmed one of their own—and these men he now faced would know that. It was a weak hand, but one he had to play out.

Ketchum nodded a casual greeting. "You make more racket than a cavalry troop, Olive," he said. "And you're a little off your home range."

Bob pinned Ketchum's eyes with a hard glare. *The damn fool's laughing at me,* he thought. The embers of anger flared anew in his gut. "Those are Olive cattle you're trailing, Ketchum," he said bluntly.

Ketchum grinned. "You're wrong there, Olive. I got a bill of sale for them right here in my pocket. Your brother's signature is on it. I'm just moving them to market for the buyer." He started to step forward, then stopped as one of the gunmen barked a warning.

"Ease that rifle onto the ground, Olive, and shuck the gun belt. Then I'll show you the paper."

Bob did as he was told, swallowing against the knot of helpless rage in his throat. A moment later he held the document in fingers that trembled in fury and frustration. He examined the bill of sale, then glared at Ketchum. "That's not Print's signature, Ketchum. You know that as well as I do. It's forged."

Ketchum reached for the paper, tucked it back in his pocket and grinned. "Then I reckon that's between you and Alex Farrell. He's the man who hired me drive the stock. You don't see my name on that paper." The grin faded and Ketchum's eyes narrowed to slits. "Now, suppose you just turn around and ride off, Olive. Or my friends and I will leave some coyote bait out here." He glanced at the hazy blue sky. "As the Sioux used to say, it's a good day to die. Your choice."

Bob Olive felt his lips twitch in humiliation and hate. "You haven't heard the last of this, Ketchum." He yanked his horse around and spurred toward Olive Town.

The three riders watched until Bob Olive had vanished in the distance. The man with the shotgun sighed. "Ami, I think we ought to of kilt the little sumbitch. You made yourself a mistake."

Ami picked up Bob's Colt Peacemaker in its tooled leather holster. "Aw, what the hell. It was worth it to watch him squirm." He dropped his own gun belt and wrapped Bob's rig around his hips. "Fits like it was made for me. I'll have to tell old Bob thanks next time I see him." He lifted the Colt from its holster and tested its weight and fit. "Forget Bob Olive. We've got cattle to move."

Olive Town

"Sonofabitch!"

Print Olive punctuated the oath by slamming a clenched fist into the table of the saloon. The impact almost toppled a row of bottles. A few of the Olive hands standing at the bar glanced at Print and quickly turned away. Print was well into his second bottle, watery eyed drunk, and getting meaner by the minute.

"We'll by God hang 'em this time!" Print's voice carried loud over the subdued murmur of conversation in the small drinking establishment. He didn't notice that one of the drifters who sometimes frequented the bar had edged a bit closer. "Ketchum and Mitchell are gonna burn in hell for this!"

Deacon Scruggs sat at Print's right, his brow furrowed in worry. Print was working himself into a killing rage. That had never taken much. The pistol-whipping he had laid on Alex Farrell hadn't taken the edge from his fury. The broken and bleeding settler had begged for his life, swearing on his mother's grave that Ami Ketchum had forced him to draw up the bogus bill of sale at gunpoint. Print would have killed him on the spot. Deacon had been able to convince him the man might be more valuable as a witness, if needed, than dead. Print had reamed Deacon out good for butting in, but the settler was still alive. Barely.

"Where the hell is Ira?" Print stormed. "Dammit, he ought to be here!"

"Easy, Print," Deacon said softly. "Somebody has to mind the cattle."

Print squinted around the room. "How many hands we got here?"

"Five."

Print snorted. "Ain't enough. Tomorrow we'll get a dozen men together. We'll stomp us some snakes on that Clear Creek outfit." Print's speech was slurred, his eyes out of focus. "Bob. Bob's gotta be in on it."

"We couldn't keep him out if we wanted to, Print," Deacon said. "He's still smarting over losing his guns to Ketchum. He'll be there."

At the edge of his vision Deacon saw the drifter who had been eavesdropping edge cautiously toward the door. Deacon secretly hoped the man would carry the warning to Clear Creek. Maybe Ketchum and Mitchell would clear out. It wouldn't hurt to burn the place, but Deacon could see little to be gained by lynching Luther Mitchell. Ketchum, maybe, deserved it. Not Mitchell. There was nothing to connect him with the stock theft. Deacon figured Ketchum was acting on his own, and he wasn't sure just how much truth there was to Farrell's confession. A man will say a lot of things when someone's whopping him on the head with the barrel of a Colt. Besides, Deacon thought with a gloomy sigh, there had been too much killing already.

Once again Deacon considered riding out. Just saddle up and leave Nebraska. Get out before a slug or a hangman's noose took him out. The idea passed. The Olives were the only friends he had. And he rode for the Olive brand. No man worth his salt turned his back on the brand. *One thing's for sure,* he thought. *There's going to be hell to pay on Clear Creek tomorrow.*

FIFTEEN

Clear Creek Ranch
November 1878

Luther Mitchell's fingers fumbled in his haste as he strapped the final harness in place on the draft team. The horses seemed to sense his urgency. The normally placid animals fought the traces, nipped at each other and pawed the ground nervously.

Mitchell glanced toward the stand of timber along Clear Creek. The drifter had said the Olives were coming; he had to get his wife and Tamar to a friend's home in Loup City, out of harm's way. Then he could worry about the Olives.

"Ami!" he yelled toward the house. "Hurry up with that trunk! It's getting light out here!"

Ami Ketchum toed open the door, a clothing trunk balanced on one shoulder and his free hand gripping a Gladstone bag. Sweat streaked his face despite the sharp chill of the morning air as he heaved the trunk and bag onto the wagon bed. He boosted Tamar into the wagon as Luther helped his wife climb over the tail gate.

Luther scrambled into the wagon seat and picked up the reins. His Sharps Fifty leaned against the footboard. He had a Smith & Wesson revolver tucked beneath his belt. Ami climbed up beside him, Winchester in hand and Bob Olive's Colt strapped around his waist.

"For God's sake, Ami! Get a move on!"

In the timber a hundred yards away, Bob Olive glared toward the wagon. "That Ketchum bastard is mine, Print," he said through clenched teeth.

Print Olive nodded silently. His head throbbed from a ringing hangover and his stomach churned in rebellion at the whiskey of the night before. Print knew he was in no shape to lead a fight this morning. He also knew that only Ketchum's death would ease Bob's humiliation at having ridden into an ambush and having his guns taken away like a raw greenhorn. "He's all yours, Bob. Go get 'em."

Bob slipped his new Colt from its holster and turned to the men. Jim Kelly's ebony face was placid and unexpressive as he turned the cylinder of his handgun, checking the loads. Deacon Scruggs sat astride his big bay, a frown on his face. Bob sensed Deacon had little enthusiasm for the job at hand. Print was too sick to be of much help. The other men in the Olive crew were all seasoned gunmen. They had no qualms about killing.

"Deacon, you stay with Print," Bob said. "Jim, you and Martinez ride with me. The rest of you spread out. There's two women in that wagon down there. I don't want them hurt. If Ketchum and Mitchell decide to fight, pick your shots. Don't fire into the wagon bed." Bob's grin was tight and mirthless. "All right, boys—let's go grab some rustlers."

Luther Mitchell started as a piercing Rebel yell sounded from the direction of the timber. The thud of pounding hooves erupted in the wake of the battle cry. Luther reached for the reins, knowing it was too late; the clumsy wagon and draft animals could never outdistance the men bearing down on them astride swift cow horses.

"Get down!" he yelled at the women as he grabbed for his rifle. It seemed that half the Confederate Army had erupted from the timber line, whooping and yelling. Bob Olive led the charge, a stride in front of the other horsemen fanned out on either side.

Olive yanked his horse to a sliding stop fifty yards away, his pistol pointed toward the men in the wagon seat. "Throw up your hands, Ketchum! You're caught!" Bob yelled.

Ami Ketchum's reply was to brace his boot against the footboard and send a rifle shot toward Bob. The slug went high. Ketchum barked a curse and levered a fresh round into the Winchester. A ragged volley of pistol fire answered Ami's rifle shot. Luther Mitchell winced as lead burned past his ear. Another slug struck the metal corner brace of the wagon bed and screamed away.

Ketchum's Winchester barked again and an Olive horse stumbled. Two wayward slugs ripped into the planking of the wagon bed. Luther heard one of the women scream as he tried to control the frightened, lunging team and aim at the same time. The reins jerked as he squeezed the trigger and his shot went wild.

Ketchum worked the lever of the Winchester as rapidly as he could, sending four shots toward the approaching men. An Olive horse went down hard, rolled over its rider and lay thrashing in the short grass. Another of the attackers flinched and turned his horse aside.

"I'm going to draw their fire away from the women," Ketchum yelled over the crackle of gunfire. He jumped from the wagon box to the open ground. Luther racked the Sharps open, fumbled a cartridge from his pocket, rammed it into the chamber and slammed the action home. Luther heard the whack of lead against flesh nearby and glanced toward Ketchum. Ami cried out, staggered and dropped his rifle. His left arm dangled at his side. He straightened with a curse, pulled Bob Olive's Colt from its holster and thumbed back the hammer. Luther braced his rifle as best he could and squeezed the trigger. The heavy blast of the buffalo gun thundered almost atop the sharper crack of Ami's pistol.

Bob Olive grunted in surprise as a heavy fist slammed into his chest, almost knocking him from the saddle. The pistol and the bridle reins slipped through numbed fingers. For an instant he didn't understand what had happened. His strength faded. The earth tilted and spun, dissolved into a blur of whirling color. He felt himself start to slide from his mount. Then a strong hand grabbed his shoulder and pushed him back into the saddle. The last thing Bob Olive saw before the darkness fell was Jim Kelly's face.

Luther Mitchell stared in surprise as the Olive charge wavered and broke. Two horsemen raced back toward the cover of the timber, holding Bob Olive upright between them.

The sudden silence that descended over Clear Creek Ranch seemed as startling as the quick gunfight. Luther sighed in relief as he glanced into the wagon bed. Both women were unhurt.

"Goddamn them!" Ami Ketchum's curse brought Luther's head around. "Shooting at women, damn their souls!" Ami knelt in the sandy soil in front of the wagon, trying to work the ejector rod of the Colt with one hand. Blood dripped from the fingers of his shattered arm. He managed to eject two spent cartridges before Tamar leapt from the wagon and sprinted to his side. She grabbed the pistol, reloaded the weapon and thrust it into Ami's hand. The weak early-winter sunlight glinted from tears on her cheeks.

"Come back, you bastards!" Ketchum yelled toward the timber. "Come back and fight like men!"

Print Olive ignored Ketchum's faint challenge as he stepped from his horse and stared in shocked disbelief at the blood soaking through the coat on his brother's chest.

"He's hit hard, Print," Jim Kelly said as Print reached up to help ease his brother to the ground. "He took one square in the breastbone." Print ripped Bob's coat open. Shards of bone glistened red through the hole in his chest. Pink froth dampened the corner of Bob's slack lips. The sight sobered Print and chased the cobwebs from his brain. He blinked at Deacon Scruggs kneeling in the crisp fallen leaves beside him.

"Get the bleeding stopped if you can, Deacon," Print said, his voice a husky croak. "Then get a coat over him. He'll die if we don't get him to a doctor quick. Anybody else hit?"

"Not this bad." Kelly thumbed cartridges into his Colt. "Durbin maybe got a busted arm when his horse went down. Bradford caught one in the shoulder. Nothing serious."

Deacon grabbed a strip of cloth from a saddle bag and went to work on the wound. Seconds later he knew Bob Olive had seen his last sunrise. No man had ever survived a hit like that. Shards of the shattered breastbone had pierced both lungs; the exit wound was the size of a half dollar where Bob Olive's spine should have been.

"What about Ketchum and Mitchell?" Kelly's voice was tight and cold as he stared at Bob's shattered body.

"Let 'em go," Print said. "There's no place in Nebraska those two can hide. We've got to get Bob to a doctor. We'll deal with Mitchell and Ketchum later. If Bob dies, by God, those two will burn in hell."

In the Clear Creek Ranch yard, Luther Mitchell stood watch as his wife worked to stop the flow of blood from Ami Ketchum's shattered arm. The Olive crew had ridden away. That didn't mean they might not come back.

"How's it look?" he asked.

"Bad," his wife replied. "The bone's shattered. Ami's got to have a doctor."

"No—no doctor," Ketchum moaned through clenched teeth. "Olives'll be watching—doctors' offices. Give me—whiskey. Cut the pain—do best you can."

Ami must be hurting something awful, Luther thought, *but he's still thinking. We can't go to a doctor.* In fact, he wondered, where in Creation could they go? The Olives owned most of this part of Nebraska. The other big ranchers wouldn't help them out. *There's only one thing we can do. Run. Try to get out of the reach of the Olives. Find a sheriff who isn't in Olive's pocket and turn ourselves in.*

If Bob Olive died, he and Ami might be facing a murder charge. But surrender was the only chance they had. Luther knew there wouldn't be any trial if Print Olive was the one who caught them . . .

Kearney, Nebraska

Deacon Scruggs stood at Print's side as the undertaker tapped the final nail into place on Bob Olive's plain pine coffin.

Deacon studied Print's face in the light from a guttering lantern. It had been three days since the fight on Clear Creek, a day and a half since Bob lost his game battle for life. Print hadn't eaten, slept—or had a drink—for those three days. Print's shoulders sagged in fatigue and pain. Deacon thought he detected a hint of moisture pooled in the piercing black eyes.

"I could have stopped it, Deacon." Print's soft words were tinged with regret. "If I'd stayed out of the damned bottle the night before, Bob might be alive today."

Deacon placed a hand on Print's shoulder. "You couldn't have stopped it, Print. Not as far as Bob was concerned. He'd have gone after Ketchum on his own. All you could have done was maybe put it off for a few days."

"Maybe." Print squared his shoulders. Deacon could tell it

took a conscious effort. "Maybe not. I guess I'll never know."
Print reached into a pocket and handed Deacon a sheaf of bills.
"Deacon, you're the best friend I've had. I want to ask one more
favor of you. Take Bob back home to Texas. Get him a nice box,
a big funeral, and bury him beside Jay."

"Sure, Print." Deacon tucked the folded bills into his shirt
pocket. "I'll take care of it. And you?"

Print turned to face Deacon. Beneath the sadness, a tongue of
rage flickered in the bloodshot eyes. "I've got things to do here.
I said once before nobody kills an Olive and gets away with it.
That sure as hell hasn't changed."

South Loup River
December 1878

Print Olive loosened the cinches and resettled his heavy stock
saddle to let his horse blow after the long ride through the rolling sandhills. Steam gusted from the gelding's nostrils at each
breath in the deepening cold. The sun, small and low on the
southeast horizon, did little to ease the bite of the north wind.

Print pulled his bulky buffalo hide coat closer against his neck
and stamped his feet until feeling returned to his numbed toes.
His gaze swept the stunted brush and crisp winter bunch grass of
the sandhills, pausing to study each clump or dune that might
provide cover to a man afoot.

There was no sign of Ami Ketchum and Luther Mitchell. Print
reined in his growing impatience. *We'll get them soon enough. There
aren't that many places for them to go.*

Within hours of Bob Olive's death, Print had set the telegraph
wires humming along the railroads. Every town along the lines,
every stage depot and trading post in the Nebraska frontier,
every road or trail intersection now carried the notice that Print
Olive would pay seven hundred dollars reward for the two men
who had killed his brother.

Print and his riders fanned out across the prairie each day,
scouring the creeks and ravines for signs of life. Jim Kelly had
followed the wagon tracks from Clear Creek. Mitchell and

Ketchum had abandoned the wagon, leaving the women to seek safe havens at homesteads along the creek, and set out afoot. Print let the women go. He had no intention of harming them. He had the unspoken support of the big ranchers in the region, men who welcomed his efforts to rid the area of settlers. They wouldn't back him if a woman were killed or injured in the process.

It was enough that the two men he wanted were on foot, tired, cold and hungry. Ketchum would be in gut-wrenching pain from his wound. The other settlers had been warned that any attempt to hide, feed or help Ketchum and Mitchell would bring the wrath of the Olives down on their own heads. The two men would find no relief among their own kind, not even a drink of water.

The hunt would end soon. In addition to Print's own crew, men drawn by the promise of a hefty reward roamed most of southern and central Nebraska, riding alone or in groups. Sheriffs from four counties led their own posses, hunting the reward more than justice. Print had men stationed in every county seat for a hundred miles in any direction.

A speck moving toward him in the sandhills caught Print's eye. He waited until the speck drew near enough to take shape, a horseman moving at a brisk trot. Print yanked the cinches tight on the now rested bay and spurred out to meet the rider.

Rob Murday greeted Print with a solemn nod. "They got 'em, Print," Murday said. "Wire just came in. Ketchum and Mitchell surrendered to a sheriff's posse just north of Loup City. Said they'd take 'em to the lockup in Kearney."

Print smiled in grim satisfaction. The hunt was over. Soon they could get down to the business of skinning the carcasses. "They'll never make it to Kearney, Rob. The Loup City law's been on our payroll for a while now. I believe they've just earned themselves a seven-hundred-dollar bonus." He paused to scratch the heavy beard that now covered his chin and lower jaw. "Mitchell and Ketchum belong to Print Olive now."

Olive Town

Print Olive sat relaxed in the saddle, his forearms crossed over the big Mexican horn, and watched as the deputy and his two guards rode away. *Probably already squabbling about how to split up the money,* Print thought.

He turned to the spring wagon. The pale, washed-out sunset painted the wood of the wagon a weak gray. Rob Murday sat on the driver's seat, boot propped casually against the hand brake, his sorrel gelding tied to the end gate. A dozen Olive hands waited for Print's orders. The men spoke seldom and then only in hushed tones.

In the back of the wagon Luther Mitchell and Ami Ketchum sat hunched and coatless against the sharp but unusually still December air. Mitchell, Print thought, looked old and beaten. His chest rattled when he breathed. He coughed and shuddered from time to time. His eyes were downcast. Ami Ketchum's face was chalk white against the pain. His bullet-shattered arm had swollen to twice its normal size. Ketchum cradled the wounded limb against his chest. His gaze was fevered but defiant as he glared at Print. Both men were shackled at the wrists. *They don't look much like killers now,* Print thought. *I'm glad we caught them before they had a chance to die on their own.*

Print kneed his horse about and led the quiet procession away from Olive Town toward the northeast. Rob Murday clucked the horses into motion. The heavily armed cowboys fell in behind the wagon.

Print glanced at the fading sky. Bits of cloud drifted across the horizon and overhead. There would be a near full moon later unless the clouds thickened, he thought, but no matter. The wagon carried two gallons of coal oil and a pair of lamps, if needed for the night's work—and beneath a small canvas tarp, a full case of whiskey. The liquor was for the men. *They'll have a celebration tonight,* Print thought in satisfaction, *and for good reason.*

He settled down for the three-hour ride to Devil's Gap, a narrow ravine choked with rocks and timber in a remote northern section of the Olive holdings.

In the distant twilight a coyote yipped three times and then dragged out a long, mournful howl. For a moment Print believed the animal wailed for the doomed men in the spring wagon behind him. The sensation passed as he reminded himself that the scavenger's lonely cry was for Bob.

Devil's Gap

Print Olive waved the column to a halt deep inside the timbered canyon. Moonlight washed over the bare skeletons of cottonwood and elm trees. Fallen leaves crunched beneath his boots as he dismounted beside an ancient elm. Its thick trunk twisted slightly as it tapered upward. The eastern limb at the first fork was bigger than a man's thigh and stood almost straight out from the main trunk. *A good hanging tree if ever I've seen one,* Print thought.

"Rob, pull the wagon up under that limb," Print said. His tone was as cold as the bitter December air.

Mitchell and Ketchum, still manacled and with their feet bound in tie ropes, sat silent and stared at the thick limb overhead as Murday moved the wagon into place. Ketchum shivered, but whether it was from the fever, the raging pain in his arm or just plain fear, Print didn't know. The two captives had spoken infrequently and only between themselves during the long ride to Devil's Gap. Print idly wondered what thoughts drifted through a man's mind when he knew his time was running out with every turn of a wagon's wheels. In this case, he decided, he didn't give a damn what they were thinking. He looked at the men and saw Bob's face, twisted in agony, his life bubbling away in bloody froth.

Two Olive hands slipped hemp lariats from tie-down thongs and tossed the ropes across the limb. Two others shaped loops and dropped the crude nooses over the heads of Ami Ketchum and Luther Mitchell. The light of the bright moon illuminated the faces of the doomed men, blanching the last remaining color from their faces.

"Olive, for God's sake," Ketchum pleaded, "maybe you got a right to hang me. But let Luther go. He's old and sick and he's got a family. Tamar and Missus Mitchell need him. They got nobody else."

"Shut up, Ketchum," Print said. "You two killed my brother. I was fond of that boy."

"Olive, please—I'm begging you. Let Luther go. His family—"

"He should have thought of that before he shot Bob," Print said. "I'm getting tired of your yammering, Ketchum." He nodded toward one of the men who held the rope around Ami Ketchum's neck. "Take a couple dallies in that riata, Sanchez, and shut this man up."

Sanchez grinned, wrapped the free end of the rope twice around the saddle horn and set spurs to his mount. The horse lunged. The rope snapped taut and yanked Ami Ketchum from the wagon bed. Print listened in satisfaction to the strangling sounds, watched as Ketchum's bound feet twitched and clawed, searching for footing in the empty air beneath his boots.

Ami Ketchum was a good three minutes dying. Print enjoyed every moment of it. *He was a tough little bastard,* Print thought; *got to give a man his due.* The twitching stopped, the body twisted a quarter turn and a dark stain spread over the crotch of Ami Ketchum's pants.

Luther Mitchell sat upright and calm in the wagon as he listened to his friend die. He coughed again. Thick sputum dribbled onto the front of his tattered shirt. He stared straight at Print.

"Olive," Mitchell said, his voice little more than a gurgling croak, "you are one cold sonofabitch. I hope we'll meet in hell."

Print pulled his rifle from its scabbard and levered a round into the chamber. "Likely we will, Mitchell," he said, "likely we will."

Print raised the rifle and squeezed the trigger. The slug hammered into Mitchell's belly just below the breastbone. The impact knocked Mitchell from the back of the wagon. His legs lay on the ground, his shoulders and head held up by the noose around his neck. He was still breathing, air whistling and rattling into clouded lungs.

"Just the way you shot Bob, Mitchell." Print ejected the spent round and nodded toward the second mounted man. "Haul him up."

Mitchell's body jerked from the ground. He died faster than Ami Ketchum.

Print slid the Winchester back in its boot, pulled the makings from his pocket and rolled a cigarette as he watched the bodies hanging limp and lifeless overhead. He scratched a match across the horn of his saddle and lit the smoke.

"Rob, you can get down off that wagon now. Grab your horse and ride back with me. The rest of you boys get rid of the bodies." Print nodded toward the wagon. "There's a case of good whiskey in there. Rob, fetch a bottle for us. The rest of you boys have yourselves a good time. Just don't get so drunk you forget the wagon."

Print mounted, finished his cigarette as he took the bottle from Rob Murday's hand. He pulled the cork from the whiskey and raised the bottle in mock salute to the bodies dangling from the limb of the elm. "Have a fine trip to hell, boys," he said. "Come on, Rob. Let's go home."

Two hours later the *vaquero* called Sanchez sat cross-legged at the base of the big elm tree and swallowed the last dregs of whiskey from the bottle in his brown fist. He looked up bleary-eyed at the bodies hanging from the limb. Another Olive rider staggered to his side and handed Sanchez a fresh bottle.

"Well, *amigo*," the rider said, his voice slurred by the wallop of a bottle and a half of whiskey, "what we do with these carcasses? Ain't no demand for scalps no more. 'Specially not a couple nester rustlers."

Sanchez tried to steady his gaze. "Been thinking on that, *amigo*. These hands of mine, they fit a *señorita* fine, and a *pistole* and a good horse, but they don't fit no shovel." He paused for a pull at the new bottle. "Now, Señor Print, he say two, three times he see these men burn in hell."

His companion chuckled aloud. "Yeah. Old Satan's got himself some fresh-cut firewood tonight."

Sanchez scratched his crotch. "*Sí.* I think maybe we could help the devil along a bit, eh? Gather some firewood. We burn these two. Burn 'em up good. Got coal oil in the wagon. Besides, it grows cold out here."

A few minutes later Sanchez touched a match to the deadwood piled beneath the oil-soaked bodies. Flames exploded among the dry branches and brush. Tongues of fire licked up and two bodies became torches against the night.

Sanchez let the warmth of the blaze chase the chill from his flesh. The rider at his side gagged at the scent of burning flesh, turned away and vomited noisily against the trunk of a tree. Sanchez laughed aloud. "A fine sight, eh?" he said to the other Olive riders.

"Fine—fine sight sure enough," a man said. "You reckon old Print's gonna get mad, us burnin' up two good ropes thataway?"

Sanchez shrugged. "Señor Print, he got plenty riatas." He shook the bottle in his hand. It was almost empty. "Eh, *amigos,*" he called, "we are out of whiskey and the hour is late. Perhaps we go back home now, eh?"

SIXTEEN

Kearney, Nebraska
Christmas Eve 1878

Major Wilson Cronin, Sixth Michigan Cavalry (Retired), glanced up from his desk at the timid tap on the door of his livestock brokerage office. He wasn't expecting any holiday business callers, especially one shy about announcing his presence. Most ranchers wanting to sell or buy cattle just walked in. If they did knock, they pounded on the door hard enough to rattle the windows.

He glanced at the mantel clock and frowned as the tap sounded again, this time with more urgency. Three o'clock on Christmas Eve. He should have been home with his family an hour ago. "Come in," he called.

Major Cronin's surprise deepened as the door swung open. A young woman stepped into the room, her arms wrapped across her breast against the blizzard outside. The thin coat she wore was no match for the howling wind and heavy snow. Snowflakes sprinkled the auburn hair that fell across her shoulders. She wore neither hat nor headscarf. The major stood.

"Major Cronin?" The girl's voice sounded thin and weary, reflecting the lines that creased a forehead too young for natural wrinkles.

"At your service, miss," Cronin said with a bow. "Come in and warm yourself by the fire. May I get you some tea, or perhaps coffee?"

The girl shook her head. "I've been told, Major, that maybe you can help me. My name is Tamar Snow."

Cronin knew the name. Anyone remotely connected to the cattle trade was aware of the feud between the Olives and Tamar

Snow's stepfather and fiancé—and that Luther Mitchell and Ami Ketchum were missing after their arrests.

"I see," Cronin said. "How may I help you?" He took the girl by the elbow and led her to a chair near the fire.

"I want you to find my stepfather and my fiancé. Print Olive took them from a deputy. I am sure he—Olive—has killed them." The girl dropped her gaze, embarrassed. "I have to know, Major. I have no money with which to pay you, but I *must* know if Olive has murdered them . . ."

"Miss Snow, this would seem to be a job for the elected officials. Have you talked with the sheriff?"

"Yes, sir. Of this county and Hall County and Sherman County. They all refused to help."

Cronin toed his own chair closer to the fire and sat. "Why did they refuse?"

"Two said they were too busy. The third, and I think the most honest of the three, said he was in no rush to die while poking about the Olive ranch."

Cronin stroked his muttonchop whiskers. "I see. Why did you come to me, miss?"

Tamar Snow's green eyes gazed steadily into Cronin's. "I was told, sir, that you are a man of courage and honor. A man with a sense of justice, and a man who has not taken sides in this quarrel between the big ranchers and the settlers. That you fear no man, not even Print Olive." She lowered her gaze and sighed. "Major Cronin, you are my last hope to find Luther and Ami. I want to see that they receive a proper burial."

Major Cronin leaned back in his chair, made a steeple of his fingers and peered over their tips at Tamar Snow. His pity for the girl was strong, but she was asking him to put his own neck on the line in a matter that was none of his making. He had done business with Print Olive on two occasions. He had come away both times with a prickly feeling on the back of his neck, yet knowing he had been dealt with fairly. Cronin had both faced and commanded men like Olive during the rebellion. They were a dangerous breed, needed in wartime. Cronin understood Olive's breed and did not fear him. Respect, yes. Not fear. And there were other men like himself in southern Nebraska.

He made his decision. This girl was near the age of his own daughter when the fever had taken her. He couldn't reach Mary from the grave, but he could aid this young woman. That might ease his own lingering pain somewhat.

"I'll help you, Miss Snow. I have, of course, family commitments until after Christmas. Then, after this storm passes, I'll gather some friends and see what we can do." He hitched his chair closer. "Now, tell me where you think I might begin to look . . ."

Olive Town
January 1879

Print Olive's fingers trembled in rage as he stared at the headline in the Omaha *Herald:*

MAN BURNERS!
Alleged Rustlers Burned
Like Witches And Heretics!

The article was accompanied by a gruesome and detailed description of the charred and twisted bodies of Ami Ketchum and Luther Mitchell. The floridly irate text decried the deaths in scathing terms, named Isom Prentice Olive as the culprit and demanded his prompt arrest and conviction. The writer heaped praise on "the gallant Major Wilson Cronin, retired from valiant service in the cause of the Union, who displayed the boldness and bravery so scrupulously avoided by certain local officials, and who led the expedition deep into enemy—that is to say, Olive—territory in search of the pathetic victims, finding them in gruesome repose."

Warrants were being prepared at the moment, the article trumpeted in the final paragraph.

Print hurled the newspaper to the floor and snatched the bottle from the table. He ignored the glass at his elbow and took three long swallows from the neck of the bottle.

"Dammit, what do these weak-kneed Yankee bastards expect?" he raged. "What we supposed to do, slap these rustlers and killers on the behinds and ask 'em to please not do it again?"

Deacon Scruggs, who had returned only a day ago from Texas, bent to retrieve the newspaper from the floor. He had already heard the story of the capture and execution from the ranch hands, but only now did the sheer brutality of the deaths hit him. It was like a sledge in the gut. *This time you've stepped in it good, Print,* he thought. *Not even our friends will help us on this one.* He lifted his own glass and felt the whiskey churn in his belly.

"Print, there's going to be hell to pay now. Half of Nebraska, including some heavy law—maybe even the U.S. Army—will be coming after us." Deacon sighed. "It's worse than the Death of the Skins this time. My God, Print! How could you let this happen?" Deacon's own anger was beginning to build. He struggled to keep his voice level. "Hanging a couple of rustlers we could get away with. But burning the bodies, no. This one's big trouble."

Print Olive slammed the bottle onto the table and swept back the saddle-length buffalo coat he wore against the swirling snow outside. He patted the butt of the Colt at his hip, then shifted the holster to a more handy position. His grin was like the snarl of a lobo wolf, Deacon thought.

"What the hell, Deacon," Print said. "There aren't enough men in the whole goddamn state of Nebraska to take me. They couldn't do it in Texas, and one Texan's worth a hundred of these flatland Yankees. Just let 'em try!"

Deacon put a hand on Print's forearm and glanced around the crowded saloon. There were almost a dozen men there he didn't know. Any one or more of them could be a lawman. Or worse. Deacon had heard the rumors that Ketchum's two brothers, both crack shots with a long gun, were waiting out there somewhere.

"Print, settle down for a minute and think. Rob Murday says you had nothing to do with the burnings. Blame that on Sanchez and too much whiskey. Fire the Mexican. Go to the newspapers and tell your side, that it was Sanchez burned 'em, not you. Nobody would hold it against you to hang a thief and a killer, but you've got to clear yourself of the man-burning charge."

Deacon swallowed, then said what had to be said. "Maybe you should turn yourself in before this thing gets out of hand."

Print snatched his arm from Deacon's grip. His gaze wavered from the effect of too much whiskey downed too fast. "Dammit to hell, Deacon! You know I can stop this without even going to trial. And there's not a man with guts enough to try to take me in over it!"

Deacon sighed. "I know how you feel, Print. We can buy off a few witnesses, scare off some others. But there's something else I want you to think about. Think about what this is going to do to Louise."

Loup City
February 1879

Louise Olive tried to hold her emotions in check as she picked up the bundle of personal items from the counter of the mercantile store. She tried to ignore the cold stares and the whispers from the half-dozen other customers in the store. The clerk had deliberately ignored her to wait on three late arrivals before taking her order in a surly, spiteful manner.

She took Billy by the shoulder and led the protesting boy from the array of pistols locked under the glass of the mercantile's display case. Louise blinked back tears of frustration and hurt as she led Billy through the crowded aisles toward the street and the buggy waiting at the hitchrail. *Maybe it's the Lord's way of punishing me for lusting after material things,* she thought. *I'm a rich woman, but now it doesn't matter. All I truly want is respect and a family to call my own. I see that now . . .*

Louise had been totally unprepared for the avalanche of hate and disdain unleashed on her and her family after the deaths of Mitchell and Ketchum. Again she found herself shunned by the women of the town and the congregation of the church she loved. She was excluded from all social events anywhere in southern or central Nebraska. She could count on one hand the friends who had stood by her, all wives of ranchers whose holdings were as extensive as her husband's.

What cut even more deeply were the letters and the lurid newspaper stories. The story of the burnings had been carried in every newspaper in Nebraska and most of the major papers across the nation. Every day, it seemed, the mail brought letters. Many came from outside the state. The tone of the letters ranged from promises that the writer would pray for the soul of the Olives to threats to burn the Olive home ". . . and see how you like it, bitch in the den of coyotes." Almost none of the letters were signed.

The newspapers were, in their own way, worse than the letters. There were frequent references to the "Olive Gang," to the "terror inflicted on innocent homesteaders," to the outright call for the countryside to take up arms "and deliver unto the Olives that fate they have so quickly handed those with the courage to stand up to these vicious transplants from Texas."

Louise had come to dread the mail trains and necessary trips to town. She yearned for the lonely solitude of her home. She stepped into the street, glanced at the buggy and almost cried out aloud in dismay.

Printed in crude block letters in red paint on the side of the new black buggy were the hated words: MAN BURNERS.

Louise sagged against the hitchrail and let the tears flow.

"Get me a gun, Ma," Billy said in his bitter child's voice. "I'll shoot any sonofabitch who tries to paint on our buggy again."

Louise dabbed a lace handkerchief across her cheeks and turned to her son. "That's not the answer, Billy," she said. "It's guns that brought us all this shame in the first place. And watch your language. I'll not have you cursing like a teamster."

She climbed into the buggy, smearing red paint onto her dress in the process, and waited until Billy had unhitched the mare and taken his seat. "Just give me a gun—"

Louise lost control. She grabbed her son by the back of the collar and shook him, hard. "Billy, so help me God, if you ever mention guns to me again, I—I'll . . ." Her voice failed as the open sobs began again. The main street of Loup City was a watery blur as Billy, surly and furious, whipped the mare into a swift trot toward home.

By the time Olive Town came into view, Louise Olive had regained her composure. There was one option open to her. She could leave Print. She could save Billy. Get him away from his father, away from the violence that followed Print, away from guns, away from rustlers and killings and hangings and corpse burnings. Print kept cash in his desk for buying cattle and horses. When the time was right she could pack a couple of bags, take the money from the desk and catch the next train headed east toward civilization. If she could find the courage.

Louise wondered if Print would even be sad to see her leave. He had never loved her—or at least he had never told her so—and now, with the trouble over the Ketchum and Mitchell thing, he was abusively drunk most of the time and unpredictable even when he was sober.

The thought of leaving Print tore at Louise's heart. She still loved him. *God help me,* she prayed silently, *I'll always love him; it's my cross to bear to the grave. All I ask is that You give me the strength to do what I must do when the time comes.*

Kearney
March 1879

Major Wilson Cronin drummed his fingers impatiently on the horn of his saddle. It would be a long ride to Olive Town. And somewhere to the east, a Union Pacific locomotive would be chugging toward Print Olive's home town. On the train were four men, all good with a gun—much like the four riders who trailed the major as he rode through the warm sun and its promise of springtime. Two others were riding in from the west. Ten men with one goal, the arrest of Isom Prentice Olive.

Major Cronin ran through his plan once more in his mind and still found no flaws. *With luck,* he thought, *I can pull this off with no one getting hurt.*

Wilson Cronin didn't kid himself that this expedition was purely one of humanitarian motives or a sense of justice. Tamar Snow's visit and the subsequent gruesome discovery of the bodies in Devil's Gap had started Cronin to thinking. Public opinion now ran heavily against the Texan, at least on a statewide basis. The man who brought Print Olive to justice would have a leg up toward a judgeship. Maybe even the statehouse. That was a matter not to be taken lightly.

He turned in the saddle to survey the small group of riders in his wake. Three had purely personal stakes in the venture. Two were the brothers of Ami Ketchum, the third a relative of Tamar Snow. The fourth was a former Texas trail hand, a hired gun who feared no man. All carried badges, deputized to make the arrest after three county sheriffs had refused to accept a warrant for Olive.

Leading the party aboard the train was Judge Eldon Barker. Cronin considered Barker to be as deadly as the hired gun from Texas, a fearless man who truly believed in justice. That the Olive case could add considerable luster to his own political future was not lost on Barker. The judge already was something of a legend in Nebraska. He always carried a pair of Colt revolvers, even into the courtroom when he presided over a trial, one pistol on each side of the notepad and gavel. There had never been a serious disruption of a trial in Judge Barker's court.

If anybody can take Print Olive, Cronin thought, *it will be this group.*

Olive Town

Print Olive stood at the mail window of the combination railway depot and post office, thumbing through the letters, livestock reports and newspapers that had rumbled into town on the twice weekly mail coach. He found little of interest except a letter from another rancher inquiring about the possible purchase of a dozen good cow horses. He made a mental note to ride out to the Seven X Ranch and do some horse trading, then folded the letter and tucked it under his arm with the less important mail.

"Mister Olive, good to see you again," a voice at his side said.

Print turned to the speaker and nodded a greeting. "Major Cronin." He extended a hand. "What brings you out this way? Looking for some cattle?"

Cronin seemed to hold Print's handshake longer than was

comfortable. "More than that, Print," the major said with a gentle smile.

Print became aware that two other men had stepped alongside. He pulled his hand from Cronin's, alarmed.

"Let me introduce you to some friends of mine, Print," Cronin said. "These two gentlemen are the Ketchum boys. Ami's brothers. We've come to put you under arrest for the murders of Ami Ketchum and Luther Mitchell."

Print started to reach for his Colt. He checked the movement abruptly at the touch of the cold muzzle of a pistol against his side. Print let his hand fall away from his revolver. Someone lifted the weapon from its holster. Print glared at the cattle buyer. "Damn your soul, Cronin," he said through gritted teeth, "I thought you would know better than to try something like this. All I've got to do is yell and a dozen of my men will be here before your pocket watch can tick."

Major Cronin's confident smile returned. "I doubt that, Print. You see, my men—all legally deputized—are rounding up your boys right now." He reached into an inside jacket pocket and produced a document. "I have the warrant, Print. Try to escape and my men will shoot."

Print glanced through the sooty window toward the street. Several of his riders strode toward the train, hands raised and holsters empty, surrounded by strangers. Deacon Scruggs was among them, a puzzled look on his broad, scarred face. Print knew then there was no way out.

Cronin braced himself for a torrent of curses, maybe even an attempted blow, from Print Olive as the rancher's plight unfolded. Instead of invective or violence, however, there was a calm acceptance in Olive's dark eyes.

"Well, Major, I'll have to hand you one thing. That was a maneuver worthy of any Army operations manual. A slick move. Nobody would ever have expected anyone to take Print Olive in his own town." Print nodded toward the procession of prisoners headed for the train. "The big man. With the scar across one eye. His name's Deacon Scruggs, and he didn't have a thing to do with Mitchell and Ketchum. Deacon was in Texas, burying my brother."

Cronin shrugged. "If he's innocent we'll turn him loose. This is the same way you gather cattle, Print. We round them up, sort them out, keep the ones we want and let the culls go."

A mournful wail sounded from the steam engine's whistle, Judge Barker's signal that all captives were aboard. Cronin led Print to the train. The first phase of the operation had gone well, Cronin thought. The suspects were in hand without a shot being fired. Now all they had to do was get the hell on that train and get out quick, before word spread and the rest of the Olive outfit stormed into town with guns drawn.

"What now, Major?" Print asked as the train jerked into motion. He was painfully aware of the gun muzzle pointed at the back of his head.

"We take you to the state penitentiary in Lincoln, for your own safety, until a trial date is set."

Print rode in silence as the train picked up speed. After a time he shrugged. "Major, this is a waste of time," he said. "No jury will convict a man for hanging rustlers. Especially those who shot and killed his brother."

It was the major's turn to shrug. "We'll see, Print. In the meantime, I suggest you get yourself the best lawyer in the state."

SEVENTEEN

Hastings, Nebraska
April 1879

Print Olive stretched his legs and flexed his shoulders to relieve the boredom of waiting. He glanced around the crowded second-floor court room. It seemed that no one had left when the jury retired. The spectators' gallery was still full. Armed guards flanked all doorways and windows as if they still feared a raid on the court house.

Print forced a smile of confidence toward Louise, seated in the front row between Deacon Scruggs and Rob Murday. She was in good hands. Scruggs and Murday had been freed after Print's lawyers convinced authorities the two men had been nowhere near Devil's Gap on the night of the hangings.

Ira, also cleared of participating in the affair, remained at the ranch. *At least somebody's minding the store,* Print thought. He snorted in disgust and turned to the gray-haired man at his side. "Dammit, J.D.," he said, "I don't understand why it's taking them so long to decide to cut me loose. A man's got a right to kill rustlers. I shouldn't even be here in the first place."

J. D. Ainsworth, lead attorney for the defense, sighed heavily. "Print, what do I have to say to convince you that you're not on trial for killing rustlers? You're on trial for burning two men. That puts this case on a whole new page of law." Ainsworth pulled a pen knife from his pocket and shaved a point onto a pencil. "Be patient. One thing you can't do in a court of law is hurry a jury. They'll be back in their own good time."

Ainsworth heaved his considerable bulk from his chair and wandered to a window. The court was in recess while the jury deliberated, so there was no reason to remain in the hard wooden chair.

The attorney stared from the window at the clusters of people on Hastings' main street. *Never saw a town so riled up over a simple murder trial,* he thought. *But then it's not often someone like Print Olive goes before a jury.*

Rumors of death threats, paid-off witnesses and the fear of a wholesale raid by Olive cowboys on the town had the locals nervous, the lawyer mused. The whole state was jumpy, in fact. Even the governor was spooked. He had asked for help and General George Crook had dispatched a hundred soldiers to Hastings for the duration of the trial. Public opinion ran high against the defendant, but Print Olive had money, power and a reputation as a man not to be antagonized. He also had the support, spoken or otherwise, of most of the big ranchers in Nebraska.

Regardless of how it turned out, Ainsworth thought, he had given it his best effort. And his law firm was guaranteed its most profitable year ever. Print Olive's money spent as well as anybody else's.

A call from the bailiff sent a murmur of tense expectation through the court room. The jury had reached a verdict . . .

Print Olive stood in stunned disbelief before the bench. He had the strange feeling he was a spectator, standing beside someone else, detached from his own body. *This can't be happening,* he thought. *It just can't be.*

"Isom Prentice Olive, you have been found guilty of murder in the second degree," the judge said, his gaze locked on Print's face. "It is the duty of this court to pronounce sentence. You will be transported to the Nebraska state penitentiary, where you will serve a term of life in prison at hard labor."

A mutter of astonishment rippled through the crowd. A few of the hangers-on cheered, but quickly fell silent under the cold stares of the Olive riders present. The judge cracked his gavel with an air of finality. "This case is concluded," he declared. "Bailiff, return the prisoner to his cell."

A bailiff carrying handcuffs and leg irons approached Print, accompanied by a deputy with a shotgun. Print stared in shock as the irons clamped about his wrists and ankles.

As they started to lead him away Print turned to his attorney. "J.D., you've got to get me out of this."

Ainsworth nodded. "I'll start the appeal, Print. We'll find a way to get you out." He glanced at the deputy and bailiff. "May I have a moment alone with my client?"

The two officers withdrew a few paces. "Print, I have an idea how we can get you out of this. But I warn you, it will be expensive. Nebraska supreme court judges don't come cheap. And it will take time."

Print Olive had one last glimpse of his family before he was led away. Louise sat with her head in her hands. Her shoulders shook as she sobbed. Billy merely stared at his father, his smooth young face impassive. *I wonder if I'll ever see them again,* Print thought.

Nebraska State Penitentiary
May 1879

Print Olive sat on the hard metal bunk in his eight-foot-square cell and stared at the raw sores on his hands.

The blisters raised by the hoe handle had broken. The angry pink flesh stung as if each hand held a dozen lighted cigars. The prison guards found a high good humor in watching a onetime Confederate soldier labor in the fields beyond the prison walls, hacking and chopping at weeds alongside Negroes who had known the pain of forced labor but had been unable to adjust to freedom.

Print had tried to fight the most brutal of the guards. All he had gotten for his trouble was a wicked beating and a week in solitary confinement on quarter rations. The man who once commanded an army of cowboys and an empire of grassland now was reduced to grubbing in the dirt like a common farmer. His humiliation was complete.

He stared at his hands as if seeing them for the first time. Hands that had dealt death by rifle and pistol and rope. Hands that still remembered the feel of bridle reins and saddle leather. Hands that had touched his son only in anger for more than eight years. Hands that seldom stroked his wife's hair or skin in tenderness, only in physical need. He clenched his fists, ignoring the pain from the broken skin, and held them close before his face.

For the first time since age ten, Isom Prentice Olive was close to tears of self-pity. It was the loneliness and the lack of space that hurt the worst. Print found himself shunned by other prisoners, even the wild-eyed man who had hacked his wife and two children to pieces in a murderous rage. Even in the state pen, nobody wanted anything to do with a man burner. Print realized that all his life he had been surrounded by people. Now, in a crowd of prisoners, he was alone—alone except for himself, and I. P. Olive wasn't pleased with the company.

He lifted his head and gazed toward the single high window near the ceiling of his cell. That one lonely patch of sky, with its clouds, its occasional hawk soaring overhead, its pinpricks of stars on a black night, was his sole connection with sanity. It brought back the memories. The feel of a good horse between his knees, the pungent scent of droppings in the horse corral on a frosty morning, the wind against his face as he led a bawling herd of half-wild steers, the vast expanse of open prairies.

The high square of sky also mocked him. It was near, yet so far out of reach. *Damn you, Print Olive,* he swore silently, *you've got no one to blame but yourself.*

Nebraska State Penitentiary
April 1880

Louise Olive sat at the visitors' bench, separated from her husband by a yard of pine and a double layer of heavy mesh wire.

Print's manacled hands rested on the pine a few inches from the wire. The year in prison had changed Print. His appearance worried Louise. Print had lost weight. His face was thin, almost cadaverous. His shoulders slumped. He seemed to have aged ten years in the last twelve months, she thought. His once black hair was heavily streaked with gray. The expressive black eyes seemed dull and lifeless. Part of the problem, she knew, was the constant backbreaking labor and poor prison food. The rest of the explanation for Print's condition lived only in his own mind.

The small talk had passed quickly, yet precious few minutes remained on her allotted once-a-month visitation time. Print's lawyers kept him advised of the process of the appeal. Deacon Scruggs was a regular visitor as well, keeping Print up to date on the status of the ranch. Deacon now waited outside for his fifteen minutes with Print.

"Louise," Print said, his voice soft, "I've had an awful lot of time to think in here. I realize now I've been a poor excuse of a husband to you and a sorry father to Billy. I was never there when you two needed me." He swallowed against a growing tightness in his throat. "Why didn't you leave me? It's still not too late, if you want to go. Find yourself a decent man—"

"Hush that talk, Print Olive," Louise interrupted. "To tell you the truth, I have thought about it. When you were arrested I was packing my trunk." She sighed. "I thought I had the courage to walk out on you. I didn't. But lack of courage wasn't the whole reason I stayed, Print. I've also had time to do a lot of thinking. When I took those marriage vows, I promised to stay with you through the good times and the bad. I'll keep that promise. I've also come to realize that we're both to blame for the flaws in our marriage."

Louise blinked against the moisture pooling in her eyelids and reached in a dress pocket for a handkerchief. "I was greedy, Print. I wanted too much of everything. I wanted it because I'd never had it before. That was the liquor I drank. It's no less addicting or intoxicating than the whiskey you turned to. I apologize for that."

Louise squared her shoulders and took a deep breath. "The real reason I couldn't leave was a simple one. I love you, Print. I always have and always will."

Print blinked against the sting in his own eyes. "Louise, I—" He dropped his gaze. "It's hard for me to say. I've never said it before, and God only knows I should have, but I didn't know how. I still don't." He raised his head. "I was too proud, too stubborn, to admit a need for anyone. Even you. If it isn't too late I'd like to try to say it now. I love you. I need you. If you want to leave I'll understand. If you'll give me another chance, I'll do my best to change. To be a real husband and father. I know now that money and power don't have a thing to do with the measure of a man's life or worth . . ."

Tears flowed freely down Louise's cheeks as she placed her fingertips against the double wire screen. Print raised his own manacled hands. Their fingers touched. "I'll be here when you're released, Print. And forever."

"No touching," a guard warned from his post a few feet away.

Louise glanced at the guard. "You, sir, may go straight to hell. I'll touch this man if I want to."

The guard sputtered for a moment, then dropped his gaze. "Guess it won't hurt nothin'. 'Sides, ma'am, your time's about up."

Deacon Scruggs walked in a few minutes later, plopped down in the visitors' chair vacated by Louise and grinned at the prisoner.

"Print, you look like the last coyote of a bad winter."

A slight smile tugged at Print's lips. "That coyote's one up on me, Deacon. I'm so hungry for a thick steak I'd even eat Olive beef."

Deacon chuckled and shook his head. "If there's one left when we get you out of here I'll cook the critter myself. We had to sell off another batch of cattle last week. Those lawyers of yours got no more ethics than a Saint Louis whore and they're a helluva lot more expensive."

Print grunted an agreement. "I know. Ainsworth told me they'd found something, though. Said they should have me out by Christmas. Deacon, is there going to be anything left to go home to?"

"Sure. We'll save enough for a seed herd, get a fresh start. Some of the big ranchers have chipped in on expenses. Dudley Snyder sent some Texas money up this way. You may be running low on stock, but you still have friends out there."

Deacon briefed Print on the status of the ranch. The picture he painted was not a pretty one. With the cattle and horse herds bled to feed the lawyers and buy off witnesses who couldn't be spooked, they had been forced to let several Olive riders go. The vast Olive ranch was a bare shadow of itself.

"Got some more bad news for you, Print," Deacon concluded, "as if I hadn't given you enough to make your belly hurt already. Nigger Jim's gone."

"What? Why?"

Deacon shrugged. "Nobody knows why. Or if they know they aren't saying. He just packed his possibles and rode off. I think he had a spat with Ira, but it don't matter. He's just gone."

Print winced. "I'm going to miss that man, Deacon," he said. "Jim Kelly and I rode a lot of trails together."

Print fell silent for a moment, then cocked an eyebrow at his friend. "Deacon, I've done some heavy thinking in this place. I had everything a man could want and more, and I kept pushing to get bigger and richer. You tried many a time to get me to rein in, but I didn't pay attention."

Print sighed and spread his fingers on the pine bench. "Now it's gone—most of it anyway—and I can't blame bad luck or the war or anybody or anything but myself. I screwed it up on my own. You've got a lot of sense for an old Arkansas farm boy, Deacon. Do you think a man can change?"

"Reckon so. Always heard a man was what he was, but he could be what he wasn't before if he set his mind to it." Deacon grinned. "And if you can make sense out of what I just said, you're way the hell ahead of me."

Print allowed himself a brief smile. Then the frown returned. "I've been a damn fool, Deacon. When I get out of this place, we'll start over. But this time we'll do it legally. Not with a gun and a lynch rope."

"Print, I got to say I'm glad to hear you talk that way." Deacon pursed his lips in thought for several heartbeats. "Times are changing," he finally said. "The cow business is changing. Days of the longhorns are numbered. Better beef stock's coming on the market. And I think the open range days are about done, too. I reckon we've had the best of the old days. Don't see any reason why we couldn't have a little piece of the new ones."

"Time's up, friend," the guard interrupted.

Deacon stood. "Well, Print," he said, "the next time I see you, I reckon you'll be a free man again."

Nebraska State Penitentiary
November 1880

"Prisoner Olive."

Print Olive glanced up at the guard standing just beyond the bars, keys in hand. The guard's expression was sour. "Yes?"

"Gather your personal stuff. They're cutting you loose. Some damned legal technicality." The keys rattled in the lock.

J. D. Ainsworth stood by the warden's desk while the prison official signed the documents that would let Isom Prentice Olive walk out of prison a free man, at least temporarily.

"We found the flaw, Print," Ainsworth said, obviously pleased with himself. "The case wasn't tried in Custer County where the offense occurred. The state supreme court overturned your conviction and ordered a retrial in Custer County." The lawyer offered a hand. Print returned the handshake. *A hell of a lot of my money has passed through that palm,* he thought, *but just walking out of this hellhole is worth it.*

A few minutes later Print Olive stepped through the front gate, listened to the heavy doors swing shut behind him and took a deep breath of the bitingly cold air. It smelled sweet.

In the street Louise sat in a rented buggy, bundled against the cold wind whipping through the snowdrifts. Billy stood beside the buggy, holding the reins of two saddled horses. Louise clambered from the buggy and hurled herself into Print's arms. Print wanted to sweep his son into a hug as well, but settled for a man-to-man handshake. He could make his amends with Billy later.

Deacon took one set of reins from Billy and handed them to Print. "Thought you might enjoy a horseback ride to the train station," Deacon said. "Man gets to missing the feel of a good horse under him, I'd reckon. Welcome back, Print." He stuck out a big hand. Print grabbed it, drawing new strength from Deacon's callused palm and the softness of the woman's body in his arms.

Louise finally pulled away. Print boosted her into the buggy seat and handed her the lines. He strode to the saddled horse and mounted. The leather of the saddle was cold and hard, but it felt like a woman's caress to Print. He realized then how much he had truly missed the simple act of stepping into the saddle and feeling the supple power of a horse's muscles under him.

He reined the horse about and stared for a moment at the cold gray walls of the prison he had just left. "Deacon, I couldn't stand going back in that place. And there's still the retrial. If they try to send me back, just shoot me. It would be a better end."

Deacon chuckled. "Don't bother countin' the bullets in my gun, Print. The retrial's going to be in the Custer County court. The boys and your lawyers been doing a lot of riding. I wouldn't be surprised if not one witness shows up. Could be the complaint never makes it to the docket. The county judge just got a couple of hundred prime heifers a few days ago. Just wandered into his pasture. Brought their own bill of sale." Deacon clucked his tongue. "Man sure drives a bargain. Them heifers cost him a whole dollar. By the way," he added, "your pistol's in the buggy."

Print Olive drew another deep breath of the icy air, grinned and shook his head. "Leave the damn thing there. I've been without it so long I'd probably shoot myself in the foot. Besides, it's got me in enough trouble already." He kneed the horse into motion. "You know, Deacon, I made a promise one time. That no man would ever order me around again, that nobody would ever take my guns away. I'm still not too keen on taking orders, even with the practice I got back there"—he jabbed a thumb toward the prison—"but I don't think I'll miss the guns all that much. Let's go home."

EIGHTEEN

Smoky Hill Ranch, Kansas
July 1882

Louise Olive dabbed the sleeve of her light cotton housedress across her sweaty brow, added a pinch of salt to the stew bubbling on the new wood stove and sighed in satisfaction.

She didn't mind doing her own cooking. She had even grown to enjoy it. There was enjoyment in watching hungry men attack the meals she prepared and the compliments that followed. She found satisfaction even in the mundane chore of cleaning the modest house on Print's new Smoky Hill Ranch. The house lacked the elegance of her previous homes in Texas and Nebraska. But it was warm and comfortable. Most important, it was home. Louise was finally content.

She did miss Anna Maria Ontiveros. Anna Maria's solid confidence and quick laughter were stilled now, consigned to the small graveplot in the stand of elms along the creek that wandered beside the Smoky Hill Ranch headquarters a few miles from Dodge City.

She missed other faces that she had known in Nebraska.

Ira, the quiet, solid and dependable Olive, had stayed in Nebraska to manage the Olive holdings that remained intact there, and was doing well. She also missed Jim Kelly. Beneath the menacing exterior and the ever-present pistol on his hip was a decent and caring man. Wherever he was, Louise wished him well.

A few of the original hands from Nebraska came along with Print when he decided to rebuild his fortune away from the hate and resentment that still flowed along the Platte. Louise was grateful for Print's newfound sensitivity toward her feelings. He had seen the pain and anguish dealt to Louise because of his actions in Nebraska. It had been Print's idea to move to a new state and get a new start away from the resentment and danger. Rob Murday and Deacon Scruggs were among the hands who stayed with Print while others chose to remain with Ira. Two older Mexican *vaqueros* also had made the move to Kansas. Those four constantly laughed and joked, even when they were dog tired from hours in the saddle. The Smoky Hill Ranch was a place where people worked hard but were able to relax when the work was done. It had been years since Louise had known a life free of tension and worry.

She stirred and tasted the stew, found it palatable if not terrific and returned to her seat at the kitchen table to finish her coffee.

There wasn't a lot of money now after meeting payroll and expenses. Louise had discovered, somewhat to her own surprise, that she didn't miss great wealth all that much.

There was more to life than money. She could admire the Kansas sunrises and sunsets, nurse her small flower bed beside the front porch and still have time for cooking, ironing, sewing and housekeeping. Part of the reason for her contentment was that she was contributing to their new start in life. The biggest reason for her growing happiness lay with Print.

He was actually fun to be around now.

It seemed strange to think of it that way, she mused as she finished her coffee and pushed her cup aside. Not many people would have considered Print Olive to ever be more than a hard-drinking and violent man who took what he wanted and to hell with those who stood in his way.

He seldom drank now. When he did it was only a small whiskey or two before bedtime. He touched her more, paid her small compliments and even laughed aloud from time to time. He still struggled at times with the idea that expressing love and affection was unmanly. But he was learning. Print Olive was becoming the man she had always wanted to marry.

He listened to Louise's suggestions now. Before the Ketchum and Mitchell affair and the prison time that followed he would have snapped at her, told her to mind her women's work and stay away from ranch affairs. Now he not only listened, but would agree to some ideas and patiently explain the flaws in her reasoning when she was wrong.

Print tried his best to be friends with Billy. The wall that had grown between them had cracked. It had not yet fallen. There were still disagreements between the two, sometimes even shouting matches. But even that was better than the cold, aloof tolerance they had shown for each other in the past.

Starting over had not been easy for the Olives.

When Print walked out of prison, and then out of the Custer County court a free man, they were almost broke. The legal battle had cost most of their money and cattle. The cost still astounded Louise—more than two hundred thousand dollars. She still had problems grasping an amount of that magnitude. Print often said they were back where they started, but he smiled when he said it.

In Kansas Print had found two cattlemen willing to enter a partnership. He founded the Sawlog and Smoky Hill ranches. The rangy longhorns were gone now, most of them lost in that first bitter winter with its interminable ice storms and raging blizzards. Print accepted the losses without complaint even though he had worn himself and four horses almost into the ground in the losing battle against the winter.

He had even found a way to turn the misfortune to his advantage. Where the leggy and mostly belligerent longhorns once grazed, more placid Herefords and other shorthorn breeds nuzzled the rich grass and clear water.

Print Olive had set out to be a good neighbor this time around, and he had succeeded. He and his hands helped out neighboring ranchers when they were short of hands and long on work. They helped him in return. Print even stayed on good terms with the small ranchers and farmers in the region, people he would have spat on in contempt in earlier days. He had been elected a director of the Western Kansas Stockman's Association, a position the old Print would have scorned.

Louise once again could enjoy her trips into Dodge City or Garden City for supplies. At first the residents of Kansas had been wary. The Olive reputation was known well beyond the borders of Texas and Nebraska. But they soon discovered that the new Print Olive had shed his horns and tail and accepted the family as respected citizens.

There were none of the whispers and accusing glances she

had endured in Texas and Nebraska, no epithets scrawled on her buggy. Now she was welcomed, not shunned. She had good neighbors, a supportive and active church, and a circle of close female friends.

She hummed to herself as she pumped water to heat for washing the breakfast dishes. It was, she thought, almost too good to last—

Louise started at a knock on the front door. She wasn't expecting company and Print wasn't due back from the range for another hour.

A young cowboy stepped back from the doorway as Louise swung the portal open. He swept his hat from his head, baring a shock of sandy hair. His clothes were worn and patched. He was a small man, barely five foot three, and slender, with a hawkish nose and green eyes set close together.

"Yes, sir? May I help you?"

"Hope so, ma'am. I heard in Garden City your husband was lookin' for a good cowhand. My name's Sparrow, ma'am. Joe Sparrow. And I need a job real bad."

Louise nodded a greeting. There was something about this man she didn't like, but she couldn't define what it was. "My name's Louise Olive," she said. "My husband will be back soon. Are you hungry? I can fix you something."

"No, ma'am," Sparrow said, "I wouldn't want to be no trouble. I'll just wait here on the porch, if you don't mind."

"Very well, Mister Sparrow. You may put your horse in the barn if you wish. There are feed and water there." Louise noted the drawn flanks of the leggy, thin sorrel. She had been around horses all her life and could tell when an animal was heavy with thirst.

"Thank you, ma'am, but Spud and me can get our water from that little creek yonder. We won't be no trouble." He settled his hat on his head, touched fingers to the brim in salute and mounted.

Louise watched Joe Sparrow ride toward the creek. He seemed innocent enough. He wasn't even carrying a pistol as far as she could tell. But there was something about him that left her feeling uneasy.

Smoky Hill Ranch
March 1884

Print Olive pushed his chair back from the scarred rolltop desk which served as his ranch office in a corner of the living room. The figures were looking good. The Sawlog and Smoky Hill spreads would turn a profit. Not a big profit like the old days before the Nebraska troubles, but considering the price of beef had gone down it would still be a good year.

He pulled down the slatted top of the desk, his only physical tie to his father. Print had had the desk shipped from the back of the store in Lawrence Chapel after burying Jim Olive barely a year ago. Jim now lay beside Jay and Bob in the Olive plot in the Lawrence Chapel Cemetery. Print idly wondered where his own final resting place would be. He concluded it wouldn't matter a whit to him at that point. He shrugged the thought away and turned his attention to more pressing matters.

Rebuilding after that killer winter had cut into his resources. Another one like that could wipe them out. But for now there was enough money in the bank to carry them awhile, even make some needed improvements to the place. One of those new metal windmills in the west pasture of the Sawlog would assure a steady supply of water for the stock. It would be a good investment, given the quirky nature of the Kansas weather. Rainfall ranged from too much at one time to hardly any for the whole year. One thing a man could depend on was the wind. If the wind made water, then maybe the Creator had Kansas on His mind when He made the man who made the windmill.

But that damned barbed wire that had started showing up here and there had to be the work of Old Scratch. Only the devil could sire something like that, Print thought bitterly. "Progress," he muttered. "Progress with points on it. Cut a cow critter or a horse to pieces." It also meant the final page of the open range history book had closed. If not now, then within a few years. At least, he consoled himself, he had been a part of it.

Print stood and massaged the small of his back. *Getting old,* he thought; *can't sit a horse a full day any longer without getting all stiff and stove up.* A light knock sounded at the front door. Louise swept past him to answer. Print patted her lovingly on the fanny as she walked by. *Maybe Louise is getting older, too,* he thought, *but she sure doesn't show it like I do; still a fine figure of a woman.*

"Joe Sparrow to see you, Print," Louise called from the door. Print heard the flint edge on her voice. For some reason he didn't understand and she couldn't explain, Louise still didn't like Joe Sparrow. Print had hired the man anyway, for the summer, and he'd been a hard worker and a good enough hand to keep on the payroll. Cowboys were a dime a dozen. *Good* cowboys were hard to find.

"Come in, Joe. Light and set." Print waved toward an over-stuffed chair in a corner of the room.

Sparrow settled himself into the chair and fidgeted with his hat. "Sorry to bother you, Print," he said, "but I need a favor."

"Ask away." Print reached for the pipe he'd taken up after quitting cigarettes. He stuffed the scorched bowl and listened as Joe talked.

"I've been thinking," Sparrow said. "The Sawlog and the Smoky Hill, and a lot of other ranches around here, been hurtin' for winter feed. Hay's expensive and it's hell's own time tryin' to get cowboys to grab the handle of a scythe and hay rake." Sparrow twirled his hat in his hands. "I've saved some money. There's a section of good grass I can lease south of Trail City. The Hammergrens have decided to go back east for a while, but they don't want to sell the land."

Print struck a match and fired the pipe. He knew the section Sparrow was talking about. It was near enough to Trail City, just across the line in Colorado, that hauling the grass by wagon or shipping by rail would be no problem. There wouldn't be any trouble selling it, either. Trail City was the gathering place for most of the cowmen in western Kansas and eastern Colorado. The Hammergren place carried thick, rich grass that made superior winter feed. The Hammergrens had sold him a few wagonloads, and it had kept the horses and bulls healthy and snorting through the winter snows. He cocked an eyebrow at Sparrow. "You need money, Joe?"

"Not really. I went over to Trail City last week on my day off and talked to the banker. He's willing to loan me start-up money, but he wants collateral. Except for a horse and saddle and a couple guns, I don't have much of that." Sparrow licked his lips. "I hate to ask, Print, 'cause you've sure been good to me here, and I'd have to leave to work the place. But if you could co-sign the note, convince the banker he'll get his money, I'd appreciate it. You'll get first call on the hay at my best price."

Print puffed at the pipe, thought for a moment, then squinted through the blue-gray smoke fog at Sparrow. "That's a lot of hard work, Joe. You've been a good hand here, but haying is contrary to the nature of cowboys."

"I can handle it, Print," Sparrow said earnestly. "This may be my last chance to own my own place. If I have to work my butt off, I will."

Print put down the pipe and offered his hand. "You have a deal, Joe. I'll co-sign the note. We'll go to Trail City Friday and square it up with your banker."

Joe Sparrow sighed in relief. "Thanks, Print. It'll be a good deal for us both. And I'll stand you a drink in Trail City." The wiry cowboy released Print's hand and walked toward the door. Print grinned at the spring in the man's step.

"What was that all about, honey?" Louise asked, dropping a hand onto Print's shoulder after the cowboy had gone. Her brow wrinkled into a frown as Print told her of the deal.

"I don't like it, Print," Louise said. "I don't want to see you get messed up with that cowboy. I found out he's served time—"

Print chuckled. "So have I, girl. All he did was rob a little store." He reached up and patted her hand. "I know you don't like Joe. But any man who wants to better himself enough to work at it deserves a chance. Besides, what harm could come of it?"

Louise shuddered inwardly. "I don't know. It's just that I've got a feeling about that man. He's trouble."

Print pulled her into his lap and kissed her. "And since when, woman," he said with a grin, "did you get to be such an expert on men?"

Trail City, Colorado
March 1886

Print Olive pulled a ten-dollar gold piece from his pocket and practically threw it onto the banker's desk.

"I hope you're happy now, Christensen," he growled at the man behind the polished mahogany. "You've got a lot of nerve, calling a note in on me."

Christensen removed the spectacles from his nose and squinted toward the big man standing at his desk. "Mister Olive, I'm sorry we had to do it. It's not your fault Joe Sparrow couldn't make a go of the hay farm. He paid back all the money but this ten, and you *did* co-sign the note. It's bank policy—"

"To hell with you and your bank policy, Christensen," Print snapped. "In my younger days I'd have had your hide for this. I'm still not sure I won't."

The banker raised a hand. "Mister Olive, don't be angry at me. I've a business to run, just as you do. It's no reflection on you personally. You know that."

Print felt the anger build in his gut. "I take it personally," he said, his tone cold. "And since I can't take it out of your hide, I'll promise you, by God, I'll take it out of Joe Sparrow's. The next time you see him you tell him that for me. I've done a lot of things in my life I'm not real proud of, but I've always paid my debts. One way or another."

Print spun on a heel and stalked from the bank. He strode down the main street of Trail City, trying to walk off his anger until the train for Dodge City pulled in an hour from now.

Print pushed through the swinging doors of Haynes' Saloon, his favorite watering hole. Maybe a couple of drinks would take the edge off, he thought. Haynes' was almost deserted in the early afternoon of a midweek day. Print saw no familiar faces among the sprinkling of drinkers. He gestured to the bartender and took a seat at his usual table. The barkeep, a ruddy-faced man with a perpetual grin on his face, brought a glass and a bottle.

"How you doing, Mister Olive?" The bartender poured Print's first drink after letting him glance at the label. It was prime Tennessee sour mash, not the usual bar brand.

"Not worth a damn," Print groused. "Joe Sparrow been around here lately, George?"

"Couple times last week. Dropped a hundred-thirty in a poker game in the Cattleman's Room in back."

Print tossed down his first drink in one motion, his anger fueled by the news of Sparrow's gambling loss. *So the little bastard could have paid the bank off if he'd stayed away from the cards,* Print thought. *And I didn't even get any winter feed out of the deal.*

The bartender shook his head. "Anybody but Joe Sparrow would have made a bundle off that hay meadow," he said. "He cut maybe half of it. Then he got drunk and set the rest of it afire, either on purpose or by accident. Guess it just got to be too much work."

Print's fist tightened around his glass. He picked up the bottle and pointed the neck of the container at George. "You tell Sparrow next time you see him that he owes me some money. He'd damn well better have it in his pocket the next time we meet. I don't like being played for a fool. I haven't packed a pistol in months, George, but I'm damn well tempted to start lugging one again. For Sparrow."

Trail City
August 1886

Deacon Scruggs listened to the steady clack-clack of the train wheels over steel rail joints and tried to shake the queasy feeling that seemed to grip him every time he and Print made the trip to Trail City. So far, nothing had come of the trouble between Print and Joe Sparrow, but a man never knew.

Sparrow hadn't spooked. It seemed that half the people between Trail City and Dodge had tried to warn the little cowboy not to brace Print Olive. Several, including Deacon himself, had offered to give Sparrow the ten dollars to repay Print and avoid a showdown. Sparrow bristled at the offer. "I ain't scared of Print Olive," Sparrow had said, "and it ain't the money. It's personal now. He threatened to kill me. I don't reckon he's hoss enough to do that."

Deacon wouldn't put it past Sparrow to shoot Print in the back one day. Print still didn't carry the big Colt in its belt holster, but he had started wearing a gun again. He had a Colt Sheriff's Model forty-five with the barrel cut down to three inches in a special shoulder harness. The gun rode just below his left arm beneath the linen duster Print wore on his frequent trips to Trail City.

Deacon was particularly worried about this trip. They were going to take delivery of several head of new Hereford bulls from the TC outfit west of town. And Sparrow rode for the TC now . . .

"Got to give those Englishmen their due," Print was saying over the rumble of train wheels. "They know good breeding stock. These bulls are supposed to sire calves that start out small, grow fast and put on weight like a pregnant Mexican. Deacon, we can cut our first-calf heifer losses by a quarter with these new bulls."

Deacon nodded. They had had this discussion before, but the enthusiasm in Print's tone was still contagious. Deacon glanced at Print. The dark face with its deep lines etched into the skin by years of wind and weather was further creased by Print's grin. The black eyes sparkled with the anticipation of a kid at Christmas, Deacon thought. Print Olive was more relaxed and content than Deacon had ever seen him. The Sawlog and Smoky Hill spreads were doing well and getting stronger by the year under Print's leadership. Print Olive might be a little thicker in the paunch and grayer in the hair than the man who trailed longhorns north from Texas, but he still knew cattle.

"We'll put up another windmill in the north valley at Smoky Hill," Print said. "We'll throw a few of these new bloodline bulls in with our cross-bred heifers. We can run four hundred head, maybe four-fifty, on that range with a steady supply of good water."

Deacon listened with only half an ear to Print's plans. The clack of the wheels was slowing. They would be pulling into Trail City within minutes . . .

Joe Sparrow watched the train from Dodge clatter to a steam-belching stop at the Trail City depot fifty yards from the loading pens. He swore under his breath as Print Olive and Deacon Scruggs stepped off the train.

Joe slipped the pint bottle from his saddle bag and took a long pull of the cheap whiskey. He tossed the empty bottle aside. The rest of the TC hands were busy with the quarrelsome Hereford bulls, trying to stop fights before the animals gored each other. Joe eased his horse from sight and rode down the back alley to the rear door of Haynes' Saloon. *This time I'll show that old sonofa-bitch,* he promised himself through the whiskey haze. *Making talk about how he's gonna skin ten dollars out of my hide. Callin' me a deadbeat and spreadin' lies 'til I can't even get a drink on credit. Pretty damn high-minded for a man burner and cow thief. Well, here's where it stops. Today.*

Sparrow dismounted and slipped quietly through the back door of the saloon. The place was almost deserted. Monday afternoons were most always quiet at Haynes'.

Joe strode to the bar, threw down a quarter and ordered a whiskey. He carried his glass to a table along a side wall and sat facing the front door. He slipped the Colt from its holster, eased the hammer to full cock and put the gun in his lap. Print Olive always stopped in at Haynes' for a drink when he was in Trail City.

Joe Sparrow fixed his gaze on the door. He would be ready when Print Olive stepped through . . .

Print closed the deal for the new stock with a handshake, signed the bank draft with a flourish and turned for one more look at his new acquisitions. The Herefords were solid breeding stock, well formed and young. They would make a lot of prime beef for the Sawlog and Smoky Hill outfits over the years.

He handed the draft to the TC owner and turned to Deacon. "Watch over the loading for me, Deacon. I'm going to have a quick drink at Haynes'. Buy you one or three when the stock's loaded and ready."

Deacon nodded. "I'll watch the bulls, Print. You watch your back. I haven't seen Joe Sparrow since we pulled in. He was settin' his horse outside the pens and now he's gone. I don't like that."

Print grinned and shook his head. "Damned if you're not getting more and more like an old woman in your declining years, Deacon," he said, clapping his friend on the shoulder. "Don't worry about Joe Sparrow. He hasn't got the guts to try anything. Just fret about how you're going to spend all that money these red bulls with the big balls are going to make us. See you in a little while."

Joe Sparrow wiped the sweaty palm of his gun hand against his pants and settled his fist back onto the worn walnut grips of the old Colt. He was ready when the door swung open and Print Olive stepped into the saloon, blinking as his eyes adjusted to the switch between bright sun and near gloom.

"Print," Joe called softly.

Print turned. "Hello, Joe. You got that ten dollars you owe me?"

"Gonna pay you in full, Print."

Joe Sparrow raised the gun and fired. The slug hammered Print Olive in the left breast, slammed him back against the doorframe. He staggered and went down. He fell on his left side, the pistol in its shoulder holster trapped beneath the weight of his body. His fingers were slippery with his own blood as he tugged at the gun with his free hand. It wouldn't budge.

"For God's sake, Joe, don't shoot—"

Joe Sparrow fired a bullet into Print Olive's temple.

Deacon Scruggs stood at the undertaker's side as the coffin lid closed over the body of Isom Prentice Olive. Outside a train whistle wailed, its call mournful in the bright wash of a brilliant sun.

"Damn shame," the undertaker said. "Man like Print Olive. One of the biggest cattlemen in the history of the business, a rich man and helluva gunhand, killed by a half-drunk cowboy over a measly ten-dollar debt."

Deacon Scruggs swallowed against the lump in his throat. "Yeah. It is a damn shame. But you know, Print mellowed out a lot over the past few years. I think he might get a chuckle out of it now. Outside of the army, old Print never killed anybody for less than twenty dollars."

EPILOGUE

Print Olive was buried in Dodge City, Kansas, in one of the Great Plains cow country's most expensive and best-attended funerals. Later his body was disinterred and taken to Texas for burial in the family plot.

Print's son Billy turned gunman and outlaw and killed at least two men—possibly more—before he was shot to death in 1887 in the street at Beaver City, Cimarron Strip, after a dispute over a woman. He was eighteen when he died.

Ira Olive remained in Nebraska and became a respected cattleman. He never had any trouble with the law.

Jim Kelly spent his declining years in Ansley, Nebraska. He died there in 1912.

Joe Sparrow drifted into Mexico, where he died in 1924. The author was unable to determine if Sparrow ever stood trial for the murder of Print Olive.

Tamar Snow, stepdaughter of Luther Mitchell and fiancée of Ami Ketchum, eventually married the son of a respected Nebraska judge.

Louise Olive eventually returned to Texas to live out her life, as far as the author has been able to determine.

About the Author

Gene Shelton is a lifelong Texas resident, raised on a ranch in the Panhandle. As a youth, he worked as a ranch hand and horse trainer, and rode the amateur rodeo circuit as a bull rider and calf roper.

He is the author of *Last Gun* and *Captain Jack,* Books One and Two in the Texas Legends series, as well as of two other acclaimed Western novels, *Track of the Snake* and *Day of the Scorpion.* He has been an active member of the Western Writers of America, Inc., since 1981.

A newspaperman by trade, he has been a reporter for the *Amarillo Globe-News* and the *Dallas Times Herald.* His most recent assignments were as managing editor of the *Sulphur Springs News-Telegram* and as copy editor for the *Tyler Courier-Times.* He has also written numerous magazine articles for *The Quarter Horse Journal, The Ranchman* and *Black Belt Magazine.*

He has taught fiction-writing classes at several colleges and universities in the East Texas area.